Stuck in the Seventies

113 Things from the 1970s that Screwed Up the Twentysomething Generation

Second Edition

Scott Matthews, Jay Kerness, Tamara Nikuradse, Jay Steele, and Greg White

Illustrated by
Jay Steele

D1342460

Bonus Books, Inc., Chicago

99 98 97 96 95   5 4 3 2 1

Library of Congress Cataloging-in-Publication Data

Stuck in the seventies : 113 things from the 1970s that screwed up the
    twentysomething generation / Scott Matthews . . . [et al.]. — 1st ed.
        p. cm.
    ISBN 1-56625-051-X (pbk.)
    1. United States—Civilization—1970–   2. United States—
Civilization—1970– —Humor.   3. Popular culture—United States.
I. Matthews, Scott.
E169.12.S848   1995
973.92—dc20   95-38779

Bonus Books, Inc.
160 East Illinois Street
Chicago, Illinois 60611

Second Edition

Printed in the United States of America

Additional illustrations by Brian R. Johnson

*Dedicated to
Ann B. Davis*

Contents

Acknowledgments

The following people know how much they have helped to make this book a reality, but we'd like to express our gratitude again. Many, many thanks to:

Carol Balluff, B.B., B.C.H.S. Class of '82, M. Bear, Brenda Bence, Dana Benfer, Dana-Beth Benningfield, Alessandra Bianchi, the Bowdoin Polar Bears, Timm Boyle and The Topps Company, Brett & Koali, Jane Choi, Rich Coppola, C.S. from Copeland House, Tia Cudahy, Phil Deutch, Dr. and Dr. E., Helena Foulkes, Jeff "Sadhu" Gelles, Jeff Hack, Leif Hoegh, Spencer Humphry and Corrine Johnson at Price/Stern/Sloan, Jesse, the Kerness clan, Michael Kubin, Lisa M.D., Brett and Ginger Matthews, Gail and Glenn Matthews, the Matthews/Thunberg/Salmon family, The MNF boys at Chad and Bruni's, Mod 16, the Neighborhood, N.H.S. Class of '79, Chris Pasko, Anna Pastore, the Prospect Street Gang, R.M.H.S. Class of '80, S.H.S. Class of '82, the Steele family, Odeline and Charles Townes, Tanya Townes, Kathleen Turner, Alex and Christopher and Toby White, Clare and Jan White, and the White/Mallon family.

To the wicked awesome Bonus Book dudes Aaron Cohodes, John Deneen, Berry Gustafson, and Larry Razbadouski for giving us a chance. To the *Airtime* cast and crew. And, of course, to the coolest section in the history of HBS, Section A, Class of 1991!

Preface

We sat down to write the first edition of this book in 1990. For us, the year marked much more than just the dawn of a new decade. It was a time of metamorphosis when, after ten years, millions of young Americans could finally leave behind the horrid brown cocoon of the '70s and emerge into a shiny new decade glistening with 70-less possibility. Disco was dead, Jonathan Livingston Seagull had long since decomposed in a landfill, Travolta was missing in action, mood rings darkened to charcoal, and the only real oil crisis was whether Florence Henderson would renew her contract with Wesson.

So it was that in 1990 five of us gathered to purge ourselves of the '70s legacy; to put a final stake through the heart of that most heinous decade. In writing this book we originally sought to provide a sort of generational therapy, hoping that—by reading **our** memories—others might come to terms with their own '70s angst. And it worked. We appeared on network television and radio stations across the country, did interviews with large newspapers and spoke at '70s encounter groups. Our book was helping thousands confront and accept the painful memories of their own Toughskin and Culottes childhoods.

But beware lest you become too complacent. Nature is again playing a cruel practical joke. Kids—too young to fear the '70s—are beginning to revel in the trappings of that decade. Just look around you and see: Brown is back, young mall teens wear macrame vests, Led Zep is touring (sans the great John Henry Bonham), Legionnaire's Disease is once more infecting weary travelers, the Bradys have been canonized on 70mm and Travolta . . . Travolta . . . **was nominated for an Oscar!!!**

Okay. So we're back. Our consciences left us no other choice. What follows is a revised edition of our first book, reconstituted and repositioned as an antidote for '70s veterans facing the painful reality of polyester flashbacks. We again pray that this book will provide laughter and cathartic healing from your recurring case of *Seventies Shame: 113 mistakes that should never, ever, be made again.*

Introduction

We were five very poor souls looking for creative ways to pay off our student loans. Ideas were bandied about and summarily dismissed for a variety of reasons, most of which centered on our total lack of knowledge about anything worthwhile—or at least profitable. Retail Australian clothing? It's been done. Ship live lobsters to Japan? There are prohibitive tariff regulations for crustaceans of any kind. Market a piece of granite as an easy-to-care-for pet and companion? Ridiculous, and it's already been done.

"Amazing," we said to each other in disbelief. "Imagine a market that would actually pay a premium for a rock in a box. The Seventies were a mess. Look what the decade did to us."

So we did. At long last we were talking about something we knew a bit about. Things of the Seventies seemed so distant that it took some time to realize how horrifyingly different life was back then. No computers or compact discs, no VCRs or 24-hour ATMs. Just throngs of people waiting in gas lines sporting oversized polyester shirt collars and well cultivated sideburns. No wonder they took solace in rocks.

We spent the next week in a cerebral time warp trying to bring back lists and images of those things that most typified that atypical epoch; things less of historical significance than cultural. Less Vietnam, more mood ring.

Thankfully, the five of us returned from the time warp peacefully humming the haunting melody of Barry Manilow's "Mandy." Apart from feathered hair wistfully parted in the middle and ill-fitting Toughskins that invariably rode up the leg to expose uncool brown socks dropping into very cool Adidas, we had sustained little permanent damage. Most importantly, we had returned to the Nineties with a complete compendium of the characters, events, and essential elements that made the era of our development so indescribably unique.

The next task was to determine what to do with this seemingly useless collection of memories and nostalgia. The immediate reflex was to try to forget it—memories of brown leisure suits are better left unremembered—but that brought us no closer to our goal of financial independence and personal growth. We searched for larger meanings: contemporary historians had hypothesized that the exorbitance of the Eighties was a direct reaction to the opposite forces that the Sixties had espoused. Could we extrapolate, then, that the Nineties would be in some way shaped by the character of the Seventies? Had we stumbled on something so profound that tenth grade social studies teachers would actually reference our work when discussing America in the late twentieth century?

The answer is, of course, no. To prophesy the future from a decade whose essence is captured by a white-suited John Travolta, hand extended in an ecstatic reach heavenward, is as absurd as thinking a rock in a box will sell. The grim truth became all too clear: the era that we look back on with the misty fond nostalgia of childhood and early adulthood is a cultural wasteland devoid of any and all redeeming qualities. We are a generation of blunted wits dulled at the hands of Mike and Carol Brady. We are societal mutants weaned on "Zoom," the Fonz, and Pop Rocks. We are evolution's greatest practical joke.

It was tough to recover from this somber moment of discovery. Tougher still to realize that Carol Brady was at the root of an entire generation's undoing. Perhaps this explains the mysterious disappearance of her first husband which left Marcia, Jan, and Cindy fatherless, or why she offered little maternal compassion when it was Peter's "time to change." Regardless, we sat stricken by the poignancy of the moment. Is it possible that our generation is merely a gathering of misfits, orphaned by the culturally barren legacy of a decade better forgotten than enshrined? Surely, if we think hard enough, we can identify something good that came out of the Seventies.

Our search for a redeemer came up empty. We were left with just one course: let the chips fall where they may and take a good look at those things that characterized the era that misshaped our generation and sent so many of us spiralling into years of confusion, searching for the answers to questions like "why did someone leave the cake out in the rain?" and "does aspirin relieve a boogie fever?"

Psychologists claim it's best to laugh at the things that do us the most harm, for through laughter comes a kind of cathartic healing. In that spirit, we offer *Stuck in the Seventies: 113 Things from the 1970s that Screwed Up the Twentysomething Generation*—a look back at a decade that future historians will surely identify as the prologue to Armageddon.

Then and Now

How do the Seventies compare with today? Are we better off? You be the judge . . .

Then	Now
Atari's Tele-Game Pong	SEGA's Sonic the Hedgehog
Donahue	Jerry Springer, Ricki Lake, Richard Bey, Jenny Jones, Montel Williams, Rolonda, Gordon Elliot, *et al*
NBC's "The Midnight Special"	MTV's "The Grind"
Converse and Puma sneakers	Nike Air Jordans and Reebok Pumps
Yo Adriene	Yo Yo Mann
False eyelashes	Pierced eyebrows and assorted other body parts
Drawings in the *Joy of Sex*	XXX rated videos, public access cable, and the Internet
Wrangler hip huggers, bell-bottom jeans, Toughskins, and Levi's corduroys	Levi's 501s, relaxed fit, stonewashed jeans with holes worn in the knees
Nair Lotion Hair Remover	Epilady
Seventeen and *'Teen*	*Wired* and *Spin*
Mood rings and Pet Rocks	Mighty Morphin Power Rangers
Digital or Timex *"keeps on ticking"* watches	Swatches or Swiss Army watches
Ball 'n' Chain AM radios and eight-track tape players	Sony DAT players and CD ROM
Psssssst Instant Shampoo *(Spray. Fluff. Brush. Go!)*	Shaved heads

Then	**Now**
Anita Bryant	Jesse Helms
The Rocky Horror Picture Show	*The Rocky Horror Picture Show*
Schlitz, Billy, and Shotz Beer	Zima
Five-speed, stick shift, chopper bikes with yellow banana seats, multicolor streamers and tire spokes	Twenty speed, electronic shift, mountain bikes with heart pulse monitors
Wealthy Arabs owning Fifth Avenue	Wealthy Seattle-ites owning Fifth Avenue
CB "ten-four good buddy" radios	Cellular car phones with voice mail and fax capabilities
Tandy's 64K personal computer	120MHz Pentium with 1GB hard drive, 4X CD-ROM and high-powered speakers
Captain Kangaroo	Barney
Romper Room	Corporate day care centers
Tab and Fresca	Caffeine-Free Diet Coke
"Charlie's Angels"	"Baywatch"
Dumbbells, barbells and Universal machines	Dumbbells, working out on Nautilus, Cybex and Soloflex machines
Pale, flabby bodies with no muscle tone	Lean and safely tanned bodies with less than 10% body fat
Horshak, Epstein, Boom Boom, and Vinnie	Brandon, Dylan, Donna, and Kelly

Then	Now
99¢ matinees at the local movie theater	$3.99 Video-on-demand
Hokey "Batman" TV reruns	Hokey "Batman" movies
Merv Griffin and Mike Douglas	David Letterman, Greg Kinnear, Jon Stewart, and Conan O'Brien
Hamburger Helper	Boneless, skinless, fat-free, free range chicken breast
Bo Derek	Ru Paul
Mono	Chronic Stress Disorder
Viet Nam	Bosnia, Chechnya, Belarus
Coffee	Double no-fat cappuccino with Equal sweetener and chocolate powder topping
Marcus Welby, M.D.	ER
Ted Baxter	Wolf Blitzer
Twinkies, Suzy Q's, and Ho Ho's	Snackwells
Flip Wilson	Martin Lawrence
The Waltons	The Simpsons
Kojak	Sinead O'Connor
Bob Newhart	Frasier
Zoom "Ubbie-Dubbie" Speak	Gumpisms
Moms	Au pairs
Watergate	O.J.

1. SATs

Instructions

Relax. These are not the SATs resurrected from the recesses of high school hell. You won't need prep courses or books. You won't have to fill in hundreds of little circles, double check the spelling of your name (to get your 200 points), .sit four hours straight in hard plastic chairs, listen to the same dull instructions between the test sections, and triple check your penciled circles to make sure you didn't make a stupid mistake, knowing full-well that the whole test was one big stupid mistake!

This is a different SAT. This is the Seventies Aptitude Test, designed to assess the decade's damage to your psyche with 113 questions. So kick up your heels and sharpen your No.2 pencils. Place all books, calculators, notebook computers, and notes away. Find an uncomfortable wooden chair attached to a desk that wobbles when you move. (Please do not carve your initials in the desk.) Pencils down and keep your test book closed until you are given the okay. Okay. Open your book and begin with question number one. Remember, cheat, cheat, cheat (the answers follow the test).

Warning

This trip may be hazardous to your health. If you feel the onset of nausea or dizziness, if your palms become clammy, if sharp stabbing pains begin shooting up your arms, if your chest starts to explode, if you long to play "High Wire Act" with Tony Manero on the Verrazano Bridge, if you're just drawing a blank and you need a little inspiration, you have permission to do any of the following during the test: sink into a bean bag chair, burn incense, macrame, pop some rocks, blast Donna Summer on the stereo, do the Hustle and *boogie oogie oogie,* stare at a black light poster under a black-light, dress (or cross dress) in a polyester leisure suit or hot pants and halter top, walk down a hill in platform shoes, find paradise by a dashboard light, fire up the bong or smoke a doobie, wear a unicorn charm, or blow-dry a part in your hair. If your mood ring is blue-green you're relaxed and calm and you may begin the test. If your mood ring is still black, it's broken and should be exchanged for a new one. *Good luck!*

1. *"I gave my love a cherry*
   That had no stone
   I gave my love a chicken

That had no bone
I gave my love a story . . ."

The preceding lyrics, when sung, prompted:

A. Reuben Kinkaid to fall in love with Shirley Partridge
B. Bluto to smash a guitar against the wall during a Delta House toga party
C. Florida Evans to stop paying for JJ's singing lessons
D. The awarding of the Grammy to Electric Light Orchestra in 1975
E. A love-sick, tone-deaf kidnapper to abduct Sabrina Duncan on "Charlie's Angels"

2. When Roman Stripe proclaimed in a national space advertisement, "We make pantyhose for . . ." they were referring to whom:

A. Richard Raskind, a.k.a. Dr. Renee Richards
B. Rod Stewart
C. Jaclyn Smith
D. Joe Namath
E. David Cassidy

3. Jose Eber's claim to fame:

A. Bo Derek's strands of long, knotted braids and colorful beads
B. Cher's greasy, stringy, black, cover-the-hipbone mane
C. Raquel Welch's dye jobs
D. Phyllis Diller's platinum blond wigs
E. Farrah Fawcett's winged and flipped hair

4. Where can the following be found: *Fold-ins, Spy vs. Spy, Don Martin Department, the Lighter Side of:*

A. *Ms.*
B. *Mad*
C. *The Pentagon Papers*
D. *Seventeen*
E. *Hustler*

5. The Tallahatchee is to *Ode to Billy Joe* as:

    A. Sensurround is to *Earthquake*
    B. Charlie is to his Angels
    C. Leather and studs are to *Rocky Horror Picture Show*
    D. The Verrazano Narrows is to *Saturday Night Fever*
    E. The Great Gazoo is to Fred Flintstone

6. The initials of the Jackson 5's fan magazine, *TcB!*, stood for:

    A. *The Cash Box!*
    B. *Tito Can't Boff!*
    C. *The Care Bears!*
    D. *Too Cool Bubba!*
    E. *Takin' Care of Business!*

7. The first name of Sonny and Cher's first and only child:

    A. Cherokee Nation
    B. Rob Camilletti
    C. Chastity
    D. Moon Unit
    E. Gypsie

8. The Hardy Boys female counterpart:

    A. Julie McCoy, your cruise director
    B. Jaime Sommers, the Bionic Woman
    C. Josie of "Josie and the Pussycats"
    D. Nancy Drew
    E. Dawn of "Tony Orlando & Dawn"

9. From the Seventies TV reruns: in the ending scenes of "The Flintstones," when Fred, Wilma, and pets pull up to a drive-in restaurant, what does a waitress bring to the side of their car (and tips the car on its side)?

    A. A side of barbecued brontosaurus ribs
    B. The stone tablet menu
    C. A big letter "C"
    D. A beach chair
    E. Beats the hell outta me

10. Where did the characters from "The Bobby Sherman Show" make their musical debut appearance?

A. "The Love Boat"
B. "The Partridge Family"
C. "Sonny & Cher"
D. "The Merv Griffin Show"
E. "The Bobby Sherman Show"

11. *Sledge: Instantly rids you of dust and grime and furniture.*

Grass Wax: Grass and lawn cleaner for the slickest lawn in town!

Poopsie: For those who are young.

Ajerx: The do-nothing cleanser. You gotta be a jerk to use it.

The preceding are examples of:

A. Failed products of a consumer goods company, costing fourteen people their jobs
B. Subliminal messages found in television advertisements
C. Wacky Pack stickers
D. Barbie's groceries for her little pink plastic refrigerator
E. Phony products from "Saturday Night Live" commercials

12. Actress who played Alice on "The Brady Bunch"?

A. Alice B. Toklas
B. Ann B. Davis
C. Aunt Bea
D. Susan B. Anthony
E. Johnny B. Goode

13. As of this printing, what band's original members are *all* still alive?

A. The Doors
B. Grateful Dead
C. Led Zeppelin
D. The Who
E. The Bee Gees

14. Name the most horrifying natural disaster from the Seventies:

    A. A tidal wave capsizing a cruise ship
    B. An earthquake destroying Los Angeles in Sensurround
    C. A meteor crashing in New York City
    D. A great white shark terrorizing the Long Island resort town, Amity
    E. Phyllis Diller before her face lift

15. The object shown here is:

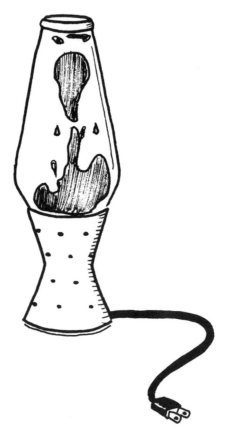

    A. A malfunctioning part in Skylab
    B. An IUD
    C. A lava lamp

D. A customized blow-dryer used to create the Dorothy Hamill
   "wedge" hairstyle
E. A bong

Mix and Match

Brady Bunch. Match the star with the Brady.

16. Eve Plumb	A. Mike
17. Robert Reed	B. Carol
18. Christopher Knight	C. Cindy
19. Maureen McCormick	D. Marcia
20. Mike Lookinland	E. Peter
21. Florence Henderson	F. Jan
22. Susan Olsen	G. Bobby
23. Barry Williams	H. Greg

Match the members of KISS with the appropriate attributes.

24. Gene Simmons
25. Paul Stanley
26. Peter Criss
27. Ace Frehley

A. Taurus. Space cadet.
   His ancestors came
   from another planet.
B. Sagittarius. Cat. Raised
   by saber-toothed tigers.
C. Virgo. Blood spitting,
   hair weaving, tongue
   flicking, tarantula-belt-
   buckle wearing, vampire.
D. Capricorn. The son of
   a medieval lord.

Charlie's Angels. Match the star with the Angel.

28. Farrah Fawcett-Majors	A. Kelly Garrett
29. Jaclyn Smith	B. Kris Munroe
30. Kate Jackson	C. Tiffany Welles
31. Cheryl Ladd	D. Jill Munroe
32. Tanya Roberts	E. Julie Rogers
33. Shelly Hack	F. Sabrina Duncan

34. In the early '70s, Charles Manson released his album:

    A. "Benny and the Jets"
    B. "Live and Let Die"
    C. "Baby, Baby Don't Get Hooked On Me"
    D. "A Slice of Heaven"
    E. "Lie"

35. Which '70s X-rated flick won the Oscar for Best Picture.

    A. *Kramer Does Kramer*
    B. *Midnight Cowboy*
    C. *Little Big Man*
    D. *The Muppets Do Manhattan*
    E. *Everything You Always Wanted to Know About Sex (But Were Afraid to Ask)*

36. What did Kalso Systems introduce to the U.S. to cure bad backs, increase blood circulation, and relieve bunion pain?

    A. Clackers
    B. Platform Shoes
    C. 2000 Flushes
    D. Unicorn Charms
    E. Negative heel Earth Shoes

37. In May 1970, name the television show banned by the State of Mississippi.

    A. "Sesame Street"
    B. "Fat Albert and the Cosby Kids"
    C. "Julia"
    D. "Love, American Style"
    E. "Nanny and the Professor"

38. In July 1970, J. Edgar Hoover's FBI named the black group, _____, as the "most dangerous and extremist prone" group of the year.

    A. Sly and the Family Stone

B. The Pointer Sisters
C. The Osmonds
D. The Spinners
E. The Black Panthers

39. Who are Hsing-Hsing and Ling-Ling?

A. Tony Orlando's back-up singers, Dawn
B. Silver medalist figure skaters who finished behind Tai Babilonia and Randy Gardner
C. The Chinese chess duo who beat the team of Russia's Boris Spassky and America's Bobby Fischer
D. The first Siamese twins separated at birth
E. Two Panda bears given to the U.S. as gifts from China

40. In May 1972, who released the single "Mary Had A Little Lamb"?

A. The Brady Six
B. Bert and Ernie
C. Paul McCartney
D. Shari Lewis and Lamb Chop
E. Josie and the Pussycats

41. Which sports team introduced seven scantily clad woman in the first professional cheerleading squad?

A. The Harlem Globetrotters
B. Charlie's Angels
C. The Banana Splits
D. Dallas Cowboys
E. Josie and the Pussycats

42. What did the letters in M*A*S*H stand for?

A. Mob of Army Surgical Hackers
B. Majors and Sergeants in Hell
C. Mostly Alcoholic Surgeon's Hospital
D. Military Armed Satire Hospital
E. Mobile Army Surgical Hospital

43. What was "Watergate"?

    A. Hit daytime TV series
    B. Unique birth control device of the Seventies
    C. A form of Seventies mind control
    D. The scandal that rocked the nation
    E. Rafting company from the movie *Deliverance*

44. Why did Richard Nixon declare "I am not a crook"?

    A. While commenting on a White House dinner, he actually meant "I am not a cook."
    B. He was a pathological liar, but a great elder statesman
    C. He believed he had merely "borrowed" the Democrat's secrets during the break-in
    D. Easier to say than "I resign."
    E. Everybody loves a laugh!

45. Patty Hearst, heiress to the Hearst publishing fortune, was kidnapped by which leftist group intent on redistributing America's power and wealth?

    A. The Wacky Racers
    B. Symbionese Liberation Army
    C. The Kiss Army
    D. The Van Pattens
    E. The Democrats

46. In his first public address after being sworn in as president, Gerald Ford declared that Public Enemy #1 was:

    A. Richard Nixon
    B. Bubble Yum
    C. Inflation
    D. That damn rock and roll music
    E. Slippery airplane stairs

47. While sitting around drinking beer, Gary Dahl thought up the ultimate fad. Once quarried and boxed, it sold over one million units. What did Gary invent?

A. 2000 Flushes
B. Pop Rocks
C. Mood Rings
D. Sea Monkeys
E. Pet Rocks

48. Who was Pelé?

A. Cover girl for J.C. Penney's
B. Guy who played "Tattoo" on "Fantasy Island"
C. Soccer star with the NY Cosmos
D. Back-up singer for Sinatra
E. One of the infamous White House "plumbers"

49. President Ford announced a national immunization plan for which Seventies Malady?

A. Polyester Psychosis
B. Boogie Fever
C. Killer Bee Stings
D. Legionnaire's Disease
E. Swine Flu

50. Who was the first woman to earn one million dollars-per-year to anchor the ABC nightly news?

A. Linda Lovelace
B. Mary Richards
C. Roseanne Roseannadanna
D. Dr. Renee Richards
E. Barbara Walters

51. *Variety* called it "dull and contrived . . ." but America couldn't get enough of the TV show:

A. "That's My Mama"
B. "Dukes of Hazzard"
C. "Good Times"
D. "Sanford and Son"
E. "Dallas"

52. Seventies Math: How many licks does it take to get to the Tootsie roll center of a Tootsie Pop?

    A. One
    B. Two
    C. Three
    D. Four
    E. *Crunch*

53. Seventies Math: Sue and Michael have been going steady for one month and three days. They have made out 12 times. When will Michael get to second base?

    A. When "Paradise By The Dashboard Light" plays on the radio
    B. When the lights go out in Georgia
    C. When Sue's parents let her stay up and watch Don Kirchner's "Rock Concert"
    D. When Sue learns the truth at 17
    E. When Rod Stewart declares "Tonight's the night . . ."

54. Who played "My Ding-a-Ling"?

    A. Chuck Wepner
    B. Chuck Berris
    C. Chuck Traynor
    D. Chuck Berry
    E. Every teenage male in America when the *Sports Illustrated* Swimsuit Issue arrived featuring Cheryl Tiegs in a fishnet swimsuit.

55. Who had the biggest hit in the 70s?

    A. Debby Boone
    B. Hank Aaron
    C. Cheech & Chong
    D. Muhammed Ali
    E. Amy Carter

56. When rock critic John Landau wrote in 1974, "I saw rock 'n roll's future . . ." who was the future?

    A. Nancy Sinatra
    B. Tony Bennett
    C. Bruce Springsteen
    D. The Wild Stallions
    E. Juan Epstein

57. Telma Hopkins and Joyce Vincent Wilson are better known as:

    A. Sonny and Cher
    B. Starsky and Hutch
    C. Lenny and Squiggy
    D. Dawn
    E. Unemployed

58. Boston-born LaDonna Andrea Gaines is better known as:

    A. Janet Reno
    B. Rush Limbaugh
    C. Ru Paul
    D. Donna Summer
    E. Maude

59. In "Bohemian Rhapsody," what was Queen talking about?

    A. Man's struggle with his mortality
    B. The essential conflict of love and conscience
    C. Society's loss of true spiritual purpose
    D. The triumph of technology over wisdom
    E. Who the hell knows?

60. Barry Manilow's song "Mandy" is about:

    A. His Mom
    B. His girlfriend
    C. His dog
    D. Mandy Patinkin
    E. Mork and Mandy

61. What were the Osmond brother's first names?

    A. Moe, Shemp, Larry, and Curly Joe
    B. Bob & Carol & Ted & Alice
    C. Dasher and Dancer and Donner and Blitzen
    D. Richie, Potsie, Fonzie, and Ralph
    E. Jimmy, Merrill, Alan, Wayne, and Donny

62. The song "Convoy" is referring to:

    A. "Carol Burnett Show" star Tim Convoy
    B. "All in the Family" star Carroll O'Convoy
    C. "Love Boat" Cruise Director, Julie McConvoy
    D. Country music star Convoy Twitty
    E. A bunch of trucks

63. Free from Sonny Bono, who did Cher take as her second husband in 1977?

    A. Musician Gregg Allman
    B. Ricardo Montalban
    C. Jimmy "J.J." Walker
    D. Gavin McLeod
    E. Her 14-year old cousin

64. Name the Osmonds' religion.

    A. Bahai Faith
    B. Mormon
    C. Muslim
    D. Satanist
    E. Church of the Divine Orthodontia

65. Who said "coochie coochie"?

    A. Richard Nixon (once out of the office)
    B. Henry Kissinger (for diplomatic reasons only)
    C. Deputy Dawg
    D. Charo
    E. Designer Emilio Fiorucci

66. Who underwent the most face lift surgeries in the '70s?

    A. Michael Jackson
    B. Dolly Parton
    C. Phyllis Diller
    D. Zsa Zsa Gabor
    E. Eva Gabor

67. Who was *not* considered the "new breed" of man—the Seventies sensitive man?

    A. Tiny Tim
    B. Tony Randall
    C. Charles Nelson Reilly
    D. Liberace
    E. Bobby Riggs

68. Name the product that is a "clever cleaver."

    A. Miracle Slicers
    B. Ronco's Veg-O-Matics
    C. Ronco's Chop-O-Matics
    D. The Ginsu Knife
    E. The Wonder Bra

69. Louise Brown has the distinction of being the first:

    A. Alleged love child of Elvis Presley
    B. Test-tube baby in the world
    C. Person diagnosed with Legionnaire's Disease
    D. Person wounded by falling Skylab debris
    E. Person to appear on the cover of *People* magazine

70. What is Pong?

    A. Bong misspelled
    B. A beer game played at Animal House fraternities everywhere
    C. The last name of a giant Panda given to the U.S. by China called Ping-Pong

D. A Chinese gymnast who won two gold medals at the 1976 Olympics

E. A $98.50 video game by Atari that was connected to a television set

71. What was Plato's Retreat?

A. A convention of philosophers convened in Berkeley
B. A small Greek inn west of Athens
C. A New York City sex club
D. A tenth-grade textbook banned in Mississippi
E. A famous Seventies spiritual spa

72. What were Paul and Linda McCartney arrested for on several occasions?

A. Accidentally referring to the Queen as "Yoko"
B. Plagiarizing Michael Bolton songs
C. Throwing toilet paper during *The Rocky Horror Picture Show*
D. Mixing Coca-Cola with Pop Rocks
E. Possession of Marijuana

73. What was Patty Hearst's Symbionese Liberation Army first name?

A. Phyllis
B. Pandora
C. Patrice
D. Tania
E. Gidget

74. Who is Evonne Goolagong?

A. Manager for Kool and the Gang
B. The woman who rang the gong on "The Gong Show"
C. Character on "The Groovy Ghoulies"
D. Inventor of the video game "Pong"
E. Winner of 1971 Wimbledon title

75. What was the "Thrilla in Manila"?

   A. Boxing match between Muhammed Ali and Joe Frazier
   B. Michael Jackson's first international concert
   C. Nickname for the Cuban Missile Crisis
   D. Birth of Milli Vanilli
   E. Farrah Fawcett and Lee Majors' honeymoon

76. Who declared "I'm the greatest, I can't be beat!"

   A. Tony the Tiger
   B. George McGovern
   C. Cassius Marcellus Clay
   D. The Six Million Dollar Man
   E. The Fonz

77. Who can claim: "Don't blame me, I voted for McGovern" in the 1972 Presidential election?

   A. Mrs. McGovern
   B. Richard Nixon
   C. Jimmy Hoffa
   D. The cast of "Eight is Enough"
   E. The State of Massachusetts

78 Who is Sergent Shriver?

   A. Character in the *Sad Sack* comic books
   B. Ri¢hie Ri¢h's bodyguard
   C. Police chief in the movie *Jaws*
   D. General Patton's boot warmer
   E. George McGovern's running mate

79. Who is Huey Newton?

   A. Donald Duck's wise-cracking nephew
   B. The guy in *Airport 75* who crashed his plane into the 747
   C. A member of the rock group Sha-Na-Na
   D. The first course in *Jaws*
   E. The leader of the Black Panthers

80. Who was President Nixon's tape-erasing secretary?

    A. Miss Moneypenny
    B. Carol Kester
    C. Elizabeth Ray
    D. Rose Mary Woods
    E. Rose Marie

81. Which of the following was not a ground breaking event for the Women's Movement?

    A. Gloria Steinems's *Ms.* magazine debuts
    B. The Roe v. Wade decision
    C. Ella Grasso becomes the first elected female governor
    D. *Time* magazine names ten women as Man of the Year
    E. Mattel introduces Malibu Barbie's Dream House

82. What is Gerald Ford's middle name?

    A. Donner
    B. Blitzen
    C. Comet
    D. Cupid
    E. Rudolph

83. Who were the Hair Bear Bunch?

    A. The original title for "Charlie's Angels"
    B. PBS show on after "Zoom"
    C. Nickname for Nixon's cabinet
    D. A Hanna-Barbera cartoon
    E. Next door neighbors of Sigmund and the Seamonsters

84. Sir Jonathan "Mudsy" Muddlemore is better known as:

    A. Ri¢hie Ri¢h's attorney
    B. The Funky Phantom
    C. The host of "Masterpiece Theater"
    D. The drummer in Josie and the Pussy Cats
    E. Evil Knievel

85. Who has wall safes the size of mansions, steamship aircraft, mechanical piggy banks, the largest car in the world with golden seat belts, and robots for everything?

  A. J. R. Ewing
  B. Little Orphan Annie
  C. The Bee Gees
  D. Howard Hughes
  E. Ri¢hie Ri¢h

86. Name the car that most resembles a fish bowl.

  A. Chevy Camaro
  B. Ford Pinto
  C. Dodge Dart
  D. AMC Pacer
  E. VW's The Thing

87. The tips of Partridge Family manager Reuben Kinkaid's wide ties were:

  A. 3″ above his belly button
  B. At his belly button
  C. 3″ below his belly button
  D. Trick question, he wore bow ties
  E. Trick question, he wore groovy dickeys under double-knit sports jackets

88. What is a dickey?

  A. The inspiration for Chuck Berry's "My Ding-a-Ling"
  B. One half of the slogan "Tricky Dicky"
  C. Hickey misspelled
  D. The most popular leisure suit brand
  E. A turtle neck cut-off at the chest level with no back

89. What did Jane Fonda wear in *Klute* and David Bowie wear on stage?

  A. Hot pants
  B. Mascara

C. Lip gloss
D. Spandex stretch pants
E. All of the above

90. Who did not have their own designer jeans?

A. Sears
B. Jordache
C. Gloria Vanderbilt
D. Calvin Klein
E. Fat Albert

91. Who's the "private dick who's a sex machine to all the chicks?"

A. Pepper Anderson
B. John Shaft
C. Frank Cannon
D. Mike Mannix
E. Barnaby Jones

92. What was *American Graffiti*?

A. The name of Led Zeppelin's fourth album
B. Playboy Hugh Hefner's yacht
C. Crime problem #1 in the inner cities
D. A movie that launched the Fifties craze
E. The cold war response to *Russian Graffiti*

93. Name the Ivory Soap model who turned porn actress and starred in *Behind The Green Door*:

A. Brooke Shields
B. Tatum O'Neill
C. Jody Foster
D. Christy McNichol
E. Marilyn Chambers

94. What was Arnold Schwarzenegger's first movie?

A. *Hercules Goes to New York*
B. *Reform School Girls*
C. *Brian's Song*

D. *Love Story*
E. *Gidget Goes Austrian*

95. Name the TV series inspired by the movie *Animal House.*

A. "Eight is Enough"
B. "Delta House"
C. "Three's Company"
D. "Maude"
E. "Little House on the Prairie"

96. What did the sign on the back of the Partridge Family's psyche-delic school bus read?

A. "Mafia Staff Car. U Toucha My Car. I Breaka U Face."
B. "Honk If You Think He's Guilty."
C. "I Think I Love You."
D. "Beep, Beep Yer Ass."
E. "Careful. Nervous Mother Driving."

97. Who lived next door to George Jefferson?

A. The Ropers
B. Fred and Ethel Mertz
C. Howard Borden
D. Peter Benchley
E. Mr. Bentley

98. Name the tent that Hawkeye shared at one time or another with BJ, Trapper John, Charles, Frank, and several nurses.

A. Hawkeye's Nest
B. Venus Nurse Trap
C. Hooch
D. The Still
E. The Swamp

99. Who were M*A*S*H's notorious couple?

A. Frank Burns and Hot-Lips Houlihan
B. Radar and his Teddy Bear
C. Charles Emerson Winchester and his opera albums

D. Colonel Sherman Potter and his horse
E. Corporal Klinger and his strapless gowns

100. What was Archie Bunker's job?

A. Dock Foreman, Prendergast Tool & Die Company
B. Postal Carrier until a promotion to shift supervisor
C. Taxi cab dispatcher at Sunshine Cab Company
D. American Civil Liberties Union field organizer
E. Bus Driver with Gotham Bus Company

101. In anger or frustration, what did Archie call Edith?

A. Angel-Claws
B. Weezie
C. Meat Head
D. Dingbat
E. Foul Temptress of the Dark Side

102. What bionic parts did Bionic Woman Jaime Somers have?

A. Bionic breasts and thighs
B. Bionic liver and kidneys
C. Bionic legs and ear
D. Bionic esophagus and lymph glands
E. Bionic hair and eyelashes

103. Name the three original Charlie's Angels.

A. Kukla, Fran and Ollie
B. Peter, Paul and Mary
C. Earth, Wind and Fire
D. Sabrina, Kelly and Jill
E. Tony, Orlando and Dawn

104. Why did angel Jill Monroe leave Townsend Investigations?

A. To race cars in Europe
B. To marry for a second time and settle down to raise a family

C. To become a cellist with the Electric Light Orchestra
D. To become Charlie's mistress
E. To go to the Betty Ford Clinic

105. Forest Ranger Rick Marshall and his children Holly and Will went over a waterfall in the Colorado River and ended up in:

A. Fernwood, Ohio
B. The Big Valley
C. Mel's Diner
D. The Land of the Lost
E. Studio 54

106. Lenny Kosnoski and Andrew Squigman are Shotz Brewery beer truck drivers and friends of

A. Chico and the Man
B. Starsky and Hutch
C. Sanford and Son
D. Laverne and Shirley
E. Quisp and Quake

107. In "Diff'rent Strokes" what was Arnold's favorite saying?

A. "Aaaay."
B. "Dyn-no-mite!"
C. "Sit on it, Willis."
D. "Say what?"
E. "What you talkin' about?"

108. Name TV's first interracial couple to appear in a '70s TV show.

A. Mork and Mindy
B. Tom and Helen Willis
C. Chico and the Man
D. Sanford and Son
E. Shields and Yarnell

109. Name the TV show where America heard its first "terlet" flush.

A. "Masterpiece Theater"

B. "60 Minutes"
C. "All In The Family"
D. "The Partridge Family"
E. "Little House on the Prairie"

110. Who was not a member of "The Not Ready For Prime Time Players"?

A. Dan Aykroyd
B. Jane Curtin
C. Gilda Radner
D. John Belushi
E. Richard Dawson

111. Name the creator and groovy cool host of "Soul Train."

A. Denny Terrio
B. Bob Newhart
C. Dick Clark
D. Don Cornelius
E. Don Knots

112. Kotter's Sweathogs included Vinnie Ba-ba-ba-ba-ba-arino, Freddy "Boom Boom" Washington, Arnold Horshack, and Juan _____ Epstein.

A. Luis Pedro Phillipo de Huevos
B. Pedro Phillipo de Huevos Luis
C. Phillipo de Huevos Luis Pedro
D. de Huevos Luis Pedro Phillipo
E. Huevos Luis Pedro Phillipo de

113. Who can turn the world on with her smile?

A. Nurse Ratched
B. Amy Carter
C. Phyllis Schlaffly
D. Anita Bryant
E. Mary Richards

SAT Answers

For each correct answer, add 1 point to your accumulated score, and compare your total below.

1. B	30. F	58. D	86. D
2. D	31. B	59. E	87. A
3. E	32. E	60. B	88. E
4. B	33. C	61. E	89. E
5. D	34. E	62. E	90. E
6. E	35. B	63. A	91. B
7. C	36. E	64. B	92. D
8. D	37. A	65. D	93. E
9. A	38. E	66. C	94. A
10. B	39. E	67. E	95. B
11. C	40. C	68. D	96. E
12. B	41. D	69. B	97. E
13. E	42. E	70. E	98. E
14. E	43. D	71. C	99. A
15. C	44. E	72. E	100. A
16. F	45. B	73. D	101. D
17. A	46. C	74. E	102. C
18. E	47. E	75. A	103. D
19. D	48. C	76. C	104. A
20. G	49. E	77. E	105. D
21. B	50. E	78. E	106. D
22. C	51. E	79. E	107. E
23. H	52. E	80. D	108. B
24. C	53. D	81. E	109. C
25. D	54. D	82. E	110. E
26. B	55. A	83. D	111. D
27. A	56. C	84. B	112. A
28. D	57. D	85. E	113. E
29. A			

If you scored between 100–113
     You are worthy . . . You are worthy . . .

If you scored between 75–99
     Congratulations! Either you cheated and looked at the answers (which we hope you have done for your sake) or you have some extremely deep-rooted problems and should seek psychiatric counseling. You know (and remember) too much. You are one scary dude or dudette. You fall under the classification of WALDO (We Actually

Loved DiscO). Did you belong to the KISS Army? Did you wear Hush Puppies or Krinkles? Did you allow your moods to swing with the changing colors of a ring? Did you know by heart the words to every theme song from Aaron Spelling television programs? You should be writing this book.

If you scored between 50–74

You are average. A typical Seventies refugee. What more can be said about you?

If you scored between 25–49

Did you take mind altering substances during the Seventies? Smoke a few "bones" behind the school gymnasium? Drink cases of Schlitz in the woods at the public park? Break into your parent's medicine cabinet and take your mother's birth control pills when you thought you were taking her valium? Sniff model plane liquid cement? PCP? Horse tranquilizers? Dead, nonregenerative brain cells are the only way we can explain your performance. But take heart, you're the sanest of us all. You forgot the trivial and hopefully remembered the important. Maybe you don't want to read on. It may be too painful.

If you scored below 24

Try to get your money back for this book, especially if you have never lived through the Seventies or you thought this book was about retirement in your Seventies.

2. An Ode for the Road

They've been called "land barges" and "living rooms on wheels," those enormous gas guzzlers that dominated our driveways and celebrated the absurdity of the Seventies. True Titans of the American road with the power of 8-cylinder engines, the cavernous room of six-passenger bench seating, and the strength of half the sheet metal in Pittsburgh.

Ours was a glorious olive green Plymouth Fury III with sticky vinyl seats, a trunk big enough for Jimmy Hoffa, and an ashtray full of Kent cigarette butts. (Remember when people still smoked?) It had a permanently stale, soaked-in odor that escaped with a *phssss* whenever anyone mustered up enough strength to open a door. We named her "Old Faithful" and she was.

My entire family of seven liked to ride together in a height order "Brady Bunch" line across the front seat. We needed a crane to parallel park and a crowbar to fit into the garage. "Honey, what was that?" was Mom's only reaction the day Dad collided with a VW bug. "Does it have a mini-bar?" was my date's reaction senior year while mashing in the hotel-room-sized back seat. Yes, "Old Faithful" was a glorious haven for me and my family for most of the decade.

Then came OPEC, the oil crisis and gas lines. The party was over for our Plymouth Fury III. The once majestic beast was transformed into a symbol of waste and inefficiency. My parents couldn't wait to trade it in for one of those Japanese matchbox cars. The quest for maximum fuel economy had begun.

We drove into the Eighties in our Honda Accords and Ford Escorts, but many of us left our hearts behind. To this day, I miss our Plymouth Fury III. Each time I squirm for leg room, every time I maneuver around bucket seats and a stick shift, anytime my little 4-cylinder strains to pass a tractor trailer on the highway . . . The list goes on and on.

But there is hope. In 1995, Toyota introduced the Avalon, their new mid-size flagship sedan with . . . guess what? . . . bench seating for six. Maybe the tide is finally turning. Maybe my family can someday have our own "Old Faithful" and my son will be able to cancel his Hilton reservations for prom night. We, and OPEC, will just have to wait and see.

3. The Metric System

Just after we learned how many feet there were in a yard and how many yards there were in a league, some European reminded us colonials that, in order to be "universally consistent," we had best convert to the metric system.

"It's easy," said my third grade math teacher Miss Millhauser, in a tone awash with pity, disgusted that she now had to unteach the system she had just taken pains to teach. "There are 100 *cents* in a dollar, so how many *cent*imeters are there in a meter?"

"A hundred!" we shouted in gleeful unison.

"Good. And how many *milli*meters in a meter?"

"A million!"

At this, the metric system was abandoned.

Now, when travelling in Europe, we are not quite sure if we're getting ripped off at the gas pumps and can only

Sizing up the metric system

plead legitimate ignorance when we are busted for speeding. I'm certain that it was the American Teachers Association that lobbied to confine the use of metric measurements to higher science and plastic soda bottles. And so it was that one more innovative improvement to the collective consciousness of American youth was struck down by the unyielding will of elementary school educators.

4. Pong

America was changed forever when Atari introduced Tele-Game Pong in 1975 for $98.50. Seventies kids glued themselves to the TV set for hours, entranced by the electronic blip.

Ask any CD ROM-equipped Nineties kid to play Pong and all you'll get is a scornful "SEGA!" in your face. Is today's technology *that* much better? Or were we just easily amused?

5. The Easy-Bake Oven and the End of Innocence

I remember sitting jealously on the living room carpet, watching those girls on TV play with their Easy-Bake Ovens. They were having a great time, surrounded by an array of beautifully decorated cakes and cookies they had created. Their mother, obviously impressed by the baking talent, looked on.

I knew I had to have one. This was something too cool for words—a real *live* oven that could bake real *live* food. It was more than a toy, it was a way to taste the forbidden pleasures of playing with the electric oven. And I knew I could talk Mom into it: it was a good practical way to learn and it would keep me out of the "real" kitchen. I made a strong case. Despite Mom's protestations that it was a piece of junk, I lobbied many months for it.

13 Memorable Seventies Television Commercials

In tribute to *The Book of Lists,* here is one of our own lists . . .

13. "Look Ma! No cavities!"
12. "Strong enough for a man, but made for a woman."
11. "I can't believe I ate the *whole* thing."
10. "Hey, Mikey . . . He likes it."
9. "Chow, chow, chow."
8. "You've come a long way, baby."
7. "I'd like to teach the world to sing . . ."
6. "Kind of hip, kind of now, Charlie!"
5. "Finger lickin' good."
4. "Schaefer is the one beer to have, when you're having more than one."
3. "Oh, I wish I were an Oscar Mayer wiener . . ."
2. "The Uncola."
1. "You deserve a break today . . ."

Christmas Day: Victory! I ripped off the wrapping to reveal the brightly colored box I had so coveted in the aisles of Child World. It was mine, all mine. Now *I* could spend hours baking my own masterpieces. Just *wait* 'til Mom saw what I could do . . .

What a fool.

Mom was right—it was "junk." The stupid light bulb inside never baked anything—I had to get Mom to put the cake-lets in the real oven to get them to solidify. The icing was a mess, too; it stuck to the cakes and made them come apart. And the cakes tasted like cardboard. They were awful.

I was incredibly disappointed. And furious. I thought of the perfect little cakes they showed on the TV and how happy the kids looked eating them with their mom and I realized: *they lied to me!*

6. Disaster Films

There was something really cool about watching an uncontrollable fire rip through the world's tallest building. The real hero of *The Towering Inferno* wasn't Steve McQueen, it was the fire itself, with its fantastic explosions and smoke. "Go for it!" we shouted. "Burn the crap out of another floor!" We couldn't wait to see the next pane of glass shatter as furniture flew and bodies fell 130 stories to the ground.

An even better protagonist was the jumbo tidal wave in *The Poseidon Adventure*. The suspense was great, counting down until midnight, waiting for that sucker to crash into an unsuspecting luxury liner, putting the passengers out of their misery by drowning out Maureen McGovern's "The Morning After."

And can we ever forget the killer shark that scared the "beach" out of us in *Jaws*? How about the earthquake in *Earthquake*? Let's face it, these mighty forces put Schwarzenegger's *Terminator* and other destructive beings of the Eighties and Nineties to shame. Watching the awesome power of nature crush naive humans was ideal entertainment for the violence-hungry moviegoer of the Seventies.

I remember the day when a fuel tanker caught fire in the San Diego port. The police evacuated everyone within a one-mile radius, roping off most of the surrounding area. There was a real danger that the tanker would explode, triggering a chain reaction that could potentially set half the city ablaze. My friends and I rode our bikes as close to the scene as possible, pulled out our binoculars and waited . . . "C'mon, go for it!" we shouted. "Let's see some action! Burn, baby, burn!" (It was at this point that I realized something wasn't quite right.)

You see, the twentysomething generation has grown up believing that life is one big disaster movie, thanks to the film producers, directors, and writers of the Seventies. We frolicked in the wind and rain, drinking beers and throwing frisbees, when Hurricane Gloria hit the East Coast in 1985. Some people ate microwave popcorn while watching the television coverage of the 1989 San Francisco earthquake. Others switched channels between the Persian Gulf War and the Super Bowl, seeing where the best action was. None of it seems real, so, of course, nobody really gets hurt. The magic of these early movies truly cast its spell on all of us.

I breathe a heavy sigh and pause to reflect. Then I pick myself up, drive to the video store and snag a copy of *Airport 1975*. Hey, what can I say? It's a great flick and I love George Kennedy.

7. Famous Conversations of the Seventies—Part I

MATT: Ms. Smith. Could I talk to you for a minute? I've got an idea . . .
(Matt enters the office. Closes door behind him. Sits down on the orange vinyl sofa.)

SMITH: What's on your mind, Matt?
(Matt is disheveled. His clothes are wrinkled, looks like he hasn't slept in days.)

MATT: Okay, okay, look—
(He leans on the couch arm.)
First we take these highly explosive CO_2 pellets and coat them with sugar . . .

SMITH: I'm listening.

MATT: Okay, so we coat them in sugar and paint them bright colors like purple, orange, and green—pretty rainbow colors.
(Smith follows intently.)
Then we put them into little packages and sell them to little kids all over the country. So then the kids put the rock pellets on their tongues and they close their mouths and the pellets explode. This tingles and is fun as long as they don't swallow them and die by accident. What do you think?
(Smith ponders the idea.)

SMITH: Great. Distribute through the standard drug and grocery store outlets. Fifty to sixty percent profit margin. Matt, what's the chance of death?

MATT: Slim to none. Only if swallowed.

SMITH: Good. No problem. Nice work!

> (Matt returns to his office. Matt begins to pace back and forth behind his desk. He pauses. Picks up the phone.)

MATT: Hello, Ms. Smith? I've got another idea.

SMITH: I'm listening.

MATT: We make these foot-long darts that kids can throw at each other in the backyard . . .

8. Lawn Darts

It is ironic that Homo sapiens have advanced so far, so quickly since the time of the ancient Greeks and yet still refuse to heed basic truths about mortality.

Herodotus relates a tragic tale about a king's three sons who accidentally kill each other while at play. Instead of Lincoln Logs or Big Wheels, the King gave each a spear, a sword, and a bow with a full quiver of arrows. With a pat on the head he bade them "have fun and be careful." Good advice from the bearer of such gifts.

In the Seventies, this scene was replayed countless times as unwitting parents presented their careless—if not sinister—children with heavily-weighted, aerodynamically perfect projectiles of death better known as Lawn Darts. Aiming at the target was fine for the first five to ten tosses until the holder of the darts discovered the fear that these weapons aroused in the hearts and minds of younger siblings.

Innocent weekend horseplay became bloody backyard battles when, as in Herodotus, good fun digressed into tragic misfortune and transformed loving young children into weapon-wielding warriors hungry for conflict.

Not Evel, but an incredible simulation

9. Evel Knievel

Evel Knievel transformed boyhood fantasies—and maternal premonitions of traumatic injury—into reality.

Equipped with plywood, cinder blocks and garbage cans, any driveway became the fountains of Caesar's Palace, and any three-speed, banana-seat Huffy became a specially-rigged Harley ready to fly. The introduction of a reinforced landing ramp allowed the legendary "Tiny" McKibbon to stretch the neighborhood distance record to a staggering seven garbage cans. "Tiny" paid the price for glory, though, as his attempt at eight cans from the top of a steep hill sent him so long that he overshot the landing ramp and landed with an impact that changed the shape of him and his banana seat forever.

10. The Silly String Attack

It was a brisk autumn day in Delmar, New York. Mark, Chris, and Paul felt a presence in the air, a feeling that chilled their fourteen-year-old bones. Chris looked to his two companions; they glanced back knowingly. The time had come.

The trio donned their matching vinyl-sleeved Minnesota Vikings football jackets and mounted their banana-seat, STP-stickered, Huffy bikes. Chris had been the first to purchase his jacket, liking the Viking's purple and gold colors. His deep green bike was perfectly balanced for popping wheelies, a skill which he had easily mastered.

Mark's bike was an obviously inferior shade of maroon. "If only my parents had bought me the red one," he thought, "then I could ride with Chris on equal footing."

Paul reached down to remove the Topps Baseball Cards from his spokes; the impressive whirring sound must be sacrificed today, sacrificed for speed and silence. Chris bolted down the driveway and swerved to the left, gaining speed. Paul and Mark followed in formation. Few words were spoken as the matching teenagers traveled the dirt path over the railroad tracks to the confrontation that lay ahead.

They reached Delaware Plaza just after 3:00 P.M. They rode their bikes along the sidewalk, past the Grand Union, Woolworths, and Record Town, finally parking in front of Kay-Bee Toy and Hobby. Paul disappeared inside the toy store while Chris and Mark carefully scanned the area.

"There!" Mark pointed across the parking lot. Chris turned his head to see three of their friends from school rapidly advancing on their bikes. They wore blue and gray Dallas Cowboy jackets and wielded the newest pre-teen combat weapon: Silly String, a pink chemical substance shot from an aerosol can.

Paul emerged from the toy store not a moment too soon, arming his companions with freshly purchased cans of the "String." The enemy attacked first, coating the wheels of Chris's bike in a calculated maneuver. Spray led to spray and soon all six were covered in sticky pink goop. The sidewalk and a few cars were caught in the cross fire. Recognizing potential liability, the six friends made a quick getaway back over the dirt path.

Relaxing at Chris's house later that afternoon, the boys realized the fatal flaw of their mission. Silly String had washed out of their hair and jeans, but had permanently stained the yellow, vinyl sleeves of their jackets. None of the boys wanted to face their mothers with the news, so a pact was made never to wear the jackets again.

Mark walked home that evening and hung his jacket in the back of a storage closet downstairs. There it remained for the rest of his teenage years.

11. Bug Zappers

The brutal reality of capital punishment was introduced to thousands of suburban backyard children with the advent of electric insect disposal devices. The perverted purveyors of death who developed these machines outlined the procedure in the following way:

Step 1: Lure happy insect into death chamber through use of synthetic sexual stimulus.

Step 2: Convince the convicted to make contact with the blue light for *the best ride of your life.*

The bug zapper entices its prey

Step 3: In order to entice more traffic, disguise the excruciatingly graphic sound of frying bug as the unashamed screams of earth-moving insect orgasm.

Step 4: Celebrate the no-mess wisp of bug ash as it distributes itself over the lawn as fertilizer.

Add-on options for the suburbanite who settled for nothing less than the best included a digital kill counter and a prerecorded tape loop of the last rites.

12. No VCRs

Captain and Tennille

13. Muskrat Love Will Keep Us Together

He dressed like a sailor.
She stood six-feet tall.
They came out of nowhere,
To sing for us all.
With lyrics so sappy,
And music so pure.
We think they were married,
But we're really not sure.

They sang about muskrats
And feelings so strong.
"Love Will Keep Us Together"
Was a number one song.
Then right on the heels
Of Donny and Marie,
They got their own show
On network TV.

They had finally made it,
Climbed their way to the top.
Then wouldn't you know it—
The show was a flop.
And they fell into hiding,
As fate would allow,
Leaving us asking . . .
Where are you now?

14. Seventies Sustenance

7:00 A.M.   For breakfast you gobble down Super Sugar Crisp (with two packets of Sweet 'N Low and one cup of milk), and drink a glass of Tang (leaving at least one inch of Tang on the bottom of the glass to avoid the sludge that settles). Oh, and of course you eat a Flintstone Vitamin (preferably Dino).

7:30 A.M.   Pre-school snack: Pop Rocks, Zotz, *big jerk* Beef Jerky and a Coca-Cola purchased at the little store outside the school grounds.

Food for the polyester generation

9:30 A.M.   Nutrition Period: Half-pint milk and a Marathon bar.

Noon   Lunch: neatly packed by Mom in your Wonder Woman or Partridge Family lunch box, consisting of a tuna fish or bologna and cheese or PBJ or Fluffernutter sandwich on Wonder Bread, and a scrubbed macintosh apple. If you are lucky, you can ditch the homemade lunch on Fridays (a.k.a. Pizza Day) and eat the cardboard tasting square pizzas, lacquered with red sauce and dotted with a few bits of manufactured cheese. Accompanying the pizza is a tomato and lettuce salad with red vinaigrette dressing and an apple cobbler desert.

2:45 P.M.   Afternoon snack #1: you visit McDonald's with your friends on the way home and triumphantly order *"Two all-beef patties special sauce lettuce cheese pickles onions on a sesame seed bun"* . . . Everybody! Backwards, now . . . *"bun seed sesame a on onions pickles cheese lettuce sauce special patties beef-all two,"* two large fries, and a large orange drink. Oh, and five packets of ketchup—three for the fries and two to be *splatted* on the sidewalk. If it is a hot day, you make a second stop at the 7-Eleven, buy a large grape Slush Puppie, suck out the syrup, and discard the cup full of ice.

3:30 P.M.   Afternoon snack #2: Mom has a peeled Sunkist orange waiting for you when you arrive home. You bring the Sunkist orange to the bathroom, break the orange into slices (because last time you clogged the toilet and got bagged), flush it down the toilet, return to the kitchen, and grab the Pringles, or if you're feeling particularly healthy at the moment, granola and Dannon yogurt. You sit in front of the television. *Munch . . . munch . . . munch.*

6:40 P.M.   Dinner: you have very little room for Mom's dinner consisting of tuna casserole or Hamburger Helper or fish sticks or Oscar Mayer wieners or Swanson's Salisbury Steak TV Dinner or Chef Boyardee Ravioli or Shake 'N Bake pork chops. Surely a large glass of

Carnation Instant Milk (flavored with Strawberry Nestle Quik) is resting at your napkin which still sits on the table. (Your mother tells you to put your napkin on your lap. You mumble, she looks at you, and you quickly comply.) More than likely some vegetable will be staring you in the face. (You can hack canned corn with *"Libby's, Libby's, Libby's on the label, label, label . . ."* but asparagus, lima beans, or brussels sprouts are too gross.) Hopefully, the dinner has instant whipped potatoes. You manage to eat half your dinner, and bury the other half under the mashed potatoes or feed chunks to your German shepherd under the table when no one is looking. Dessert is raspberry 1-2-3 JELLO with a mega-load of Cool Whip topping.

6:50 P.M. Evening snack: you grab the Nabisco Easy Cheese or Hostess Suzy Q's, and a Tab (because you're watching your weight), and claim your spot on the couch before the others arrive to watch Walter Cronkite. You spend the rest of the night in front of the television, digesting.

10:00 P.M. Beddy-bye: after you discard the lump of Bubble Yum that has been lodged between your cheek and gums for the last two hours and release a wicked loud burp, you let your head rest on the pillow, once again forgetting to brush your teeth. You fall asleep at 1:45 A.M. after the sugar releases its hold.

Total caloric intake for the day: approximately 5,756.

Total fat intake for the day: Who cares? You didn't count it back then.

Number of cavities at age twenty-one: thirty-two.

Life expectancy if the above menu is followed daily: thirty-five years of age.

13 Things that Made a Guy Really Cool

13. A hairy, Burt Reynold's like, chest.
12. Patches ironed on a blue denim jacket.
11. A chain with an oversized silver cross buried deep beneath at least twenty gold chains that hold various icons.
10. Fuzz above the upper-lip signalling the beginning of a mustache.
9. "Disco Sucks" and "Adidas" t-shirts
8. Wearing a concert t-shirt the day after the concert
7. Taking a radical stand on anything like refusing to stand during the "Pledge of Allegiance" in homeroom.
6. An ability to perform Denny Terrio dance moves.
5. Losing your virginity.
4. Having a close call with the cops.
3. Parents who were at Woodstock.
2. Broken limb in cast with many multi-colored autographs.
1. 23 channel CB radio with a cool handle.

15. Bionics

His bicycle hits a patch of sand and leaves Stanley on his back, scraped and dazed. He opens his eyes and gathers the strength to mutter the healing incantation: "Stanley Rosenzweig, a man barely alive. We can rebuild him, we have the technology. We can make him better than he was; better, stronger, faster."

Stanley arises and can feel the new life force pulsing through his veins. His bionic legs pedal him home to find his sister staring helplessly at a tree. He looks up. *Dn-dn-dn-dn-dn.* Yes, his bionic vision can just make out the shadow of a frisbee caught in a lower branch.

Stanley grabs a bionic stick and approaches the tree. *Dn-dn-dn-dn-dn-dn.* The bionic stick hits the frisbee and it falls to the ground undamaged. His sister is duly impressed.

"Stanley! Put that stick down immediately and come inside this instant."

Must be Oscar Goldman calling from OSI. Dn-dn-dn-dn-dn-dn.

16. WIN Buttons

When Gerald Ford became president in August 1974, he announced that inflation was "public enemy number one." (This was a bit of a surprise, since most of us thought Nixon was.) Inflation seemed to be immune to any cures the government had offered up until that time, so it certainly seemed like a formidable adversary.

Two months later, President Ford announced his solution to the inflation problem. Not wage and price controls. Not government spending. Not tighter monetary policy. The answer to inflation was buttons. "WIN" buttons, whose letters stood for "Whip Inflation Now."

Yes, we had been trying unsuccessfully to fight inflation by tinkering with complicated fiscal policies and the ever-volatile money supply, but the real answer was simple: to beat inflation, you just had to *wish it away*. The reasoning seemed to be that if people believed—really *believed*—that prices weren't going to rise, then they wouldn't rise. And the best way to get people to believe something in the Seventies was to print it up on hundreds of thousands of buttons and give them away. (Just witness the success "Elect Nixon" buttons had in 1972!)

WIN buttons became one of the shortest-lived and stupidest fads of the decade, but they have the distinction of being perhaps the most idiotic thing ever to be *presidentially sanctioned.*

17. Deja Vu

The next time you find yourself walking through a shopping mall, try this little experiment:

Locate the nearest GAP outlet or similar teen, young-adult clothing store. Walk up to the store slowly, keeping your head turned away. When you've reached the entrance, turn your head quickly and take a good look at the contents inside.

Flashes of neon yellow, pink, and green. Patches of glowing orange, red, and blue. The steady beat of dance music blaring in the background.

Does this scene look familiar? It should. The GAP store of the Nineties closely matches the teenage bedroom of the Seventies.

Let your mind wander. Think back to your collection of velvet blacklight posters—glow in the dark images of panthers, horses, dragons, and motorcycles. Remember the wood-paneled stereo with its stack of 45s on the turntable and built-in eight-track tape player.

That's right. Clothes shopping is a trip down memory lane.

What are the implications? Difficult to say. Perhaps Nineties' neon is a harmless expression of a timeless teenage passion for bright color. On the other hand, we may be witnessing the first wave of a dangerous flood; a full-blown Seventies revival may be in the works. We have clothing now, but what will be next? The green neon Boyz II Men CD Walkman? Holographic pink blacklight Madonna posters? I shudder at the thought.

Our shopping malls are glowing.

Our teenagers are glowing.

Perhaps this is what Bruce Springsteen meant when he wrote, "Blinded by the Light."

18. Malling

The following conversation took place basically every day between 1968 and 1971.

Me: What do you want to do today?

Timmy Reilly: I don't know, what do you want to do?

Me: I don't know. Want to go to Keane Park and scare the ducks?

Timmy Reilly: Okay.

Ours to explore

Somewhere in the spring of 1972, it was replaced by the following:

Me: What do you want to do today?

Timmy Reilly: I don't know, what do you want to do?

Me: I don't know. Want to go to the mall?

Timmy Reilly: Okay.

Yes, malls changed our lives. And not just because they saved a lot of wear and tear on the ducks.

In the Seventies, malls became the new domain of suburban youth. Parents didn't seem to mind. After all, shopping was a worthy avocation. And malls offered a relatively supervised environment. They were clean, enclosed from all weather conditions and not dangerous.

For us kids, malls were more than retail havens, they were a place to hang out. To explore. To own, as we own our home turf. Malls offered excitement, social interaction and an endless supply of material temptations that trained us for a lifetime of consumerism. In malls we first learned that sense of yearning for material possessions—the physical *need* that overtook us when we saw the latest Hot Wheels car in K-Mart or the new Kiddles character that we *had* to have.

When they built the Hollywood Mall less than a half-mile from my house, my life was transformed. Timmy Reilly and I went there every day. We knew every inch of the place, from Sears Garden Center to Gray's Drug Store (great candy department). We knew the instant Doktor's Pet Center got a new breed of fish and could tell you exactly how many tiles there were between one end of the mall and the other.

To this day, I still feel at home in any mall. Having spent so much of my childhood there, it's like returning to the womb, albeit an air-conditioned one. Whether I'm in Boston's Copley Place or Newport Beach's South-coast Plaza, I instinctively know my way around. And I can keep myself entertained for hours. Maybe it's because I equate mall shopping with the utmost in leisure. I still get a sense of childish wonder when I survey a fresh array of goods available for purchase. Perhaps the only real difference is that now, unlike in my childhood, I know I am no longer safe in a shopping mall, for in my adulthood I am armed with a credit card.

19. Gotta Have a Gimmick

In the Seventies, there was a surefire formula for producing a successful television series: take a detective, add a special gimmick, and watch the ratings soar.

Detective(s)	Gimmick
Sgt. Suzanne "Pepper" Anderson	Cleavage
Charlie's Angels	More Cleavage
CHiPs	Tanned Biceps
Tom Banacek	Polish Ancestry
Tony Baretta	Parrot
Frank Cannon	Portliness
Lt. Columbo	Trench Coat
Robert Ironside	Wheelchair
Barnaby Jones	Senility
Theo Kojak	Hair loss and Lollypop
Mike Longstreet	Seeing Eye Dog, Pax
Christie Love	"With-it" Afro

Joe Mannix	Technical Sophistication
Sam McCloud	Horse
Steve McGarrett	Danno
Stewart "Mac" McMillan	Wife, Sally
Jim Rockford	Answering Machine
Dave Starsky and	
Ken Hutchinson	Hot Car
S.W.A.T.	Artillery

Who loves ya, baby?

20. Lip Smackers

Root beer, strawberry, grape or chocolate? Which will Toby like the best? We're going to kiss tonight. I can tell by the look in his eyes. We held hands by my locker today. That's when I knew for sure.

Lime, cherry, lemon or banana? So many choices, so little time. It's important—the flavor. That's what Ginger says. She and Brett kissed last weekend. She was wearing coconut. She said it made all the difference. Jane was wearing peppermint just before she and Rob broke up. It's chemistry—that's what Ginger says and she's kissed lots of boys.

Tonight will be the first time. I want it to be perfect. Cola, orange or wintergreen? I've got to get this right. It's my one and only chance. Why does life have to be so complicated?

---

13 Seventies Movies We Thought We Should Mention

13. *The Exorcist*
12. *A Clockwork Orange*
11. *The Texas Chain Saw Massacre*
10. *Billy Jack*
 9. *Blazing Saddles*
 8. *Pumping Iron*
 7. *Carrie*
 6. *Chariots of the Gods*
 5. *Love Story*
 4. *Taxi Driver*
 3. *Grease*
 2. *Car Wash*
 1. *Deliverance*

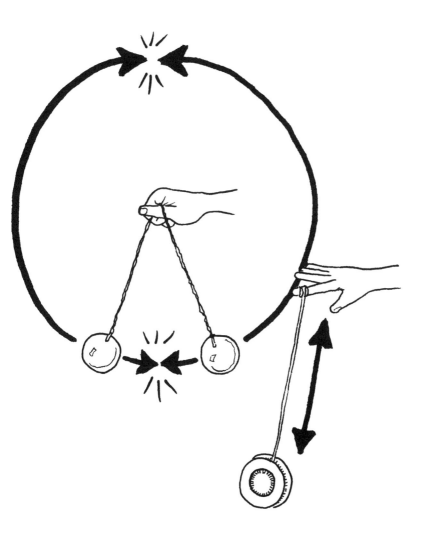

Clackers and the classic yo-yo

21. Things on Strings

Clackers.   This toy, made of two clear balls at the end of
two cords attached to a stick, was invented

for the sole purpose of making an intolerable racket. And we did.

Yo-Yos.   Butterfly Yo-Yos were best for walk-the-dog. Imperial Yo-Yos were best for rock-the-baby. Glow-in-the-dark Yo-Yos were best at night.

22. Cyclamates and the Evolution of the Alternative Beverage

In 1970, the Food and Drug Administration determined that cyclamates (a form of artificial sweetener) were poisoning America's youth. Cyclamates were swiftly removed from the market and with them went "Fizzies"—an Alka Seltzer-sized tablet that flavored drinking water. Cyclamates may have done more damage to our nation than Watergate, for when "Fizzies" were taken out of circulation, children were left with no alternative but to drink plain water.

The cyclamate curse haunts us today as the same kids that grimaced at the idea of drinking unflavored water went on to invent peach wine coolers.

23. True Teen Confessions #1: My Seventies Soul-Mate

Okay. Okay. I admit it. It has taken years of cutting edge psychotherapy (and nearly $10,000) to be able to

state this in public. Yes, I . . . I mailed in my hard-earned $2.00 in small change (plus two quarters for return airmail postage) to the J-5 Headquarters to become Michael Jackson's *Personal Soul-Mate*. For nearly two decades, I cherished my own *Personal Soul-Mate* letter written to me from Michael, my own sixty-five official *Personal Soul-Mate* letter seal stickers with Michael's smiling face on them, my own *Personal Soul-Mate* ID card signed by Michael, my own *Personal Soul-Mate* posters, and my own *Personal Soul-Mate* portrait-size and wallet-size pictures of Michael. I kept all seventy-nine (*"just count them!"*) incredible *Personal Soul-Mate* items under my bed and close to my heart. However, today I stand before you a cured man. And as testimony to my accomplishment, I have just lit a match and placed it on my pile of *Personal Soul-Mate "OUTASIGHT J-5 GROOVY GOOD STUFF."* The poster with a special *Personal Soul-Mate* poem written to me by Michael is browning around the edges now and starting to curl up . . . The smoke is getting thicker . . . Michael's hair is catching fire . . . I . . . I'm okay . . . Deep breaths . . . Oh God!!! Michael!!! My *Personal Soul-Mate* is burning . . . I'm killing him . . . I'm sorry Michael . . . It'll never happen again . . . Maybe I'll burn my Marie Osmond stuff first.

24. Driving Role Models

There is little wonder why people of our generation can't drive 55. Our heroes drove fast. Beginning with "Speed Racer" and "Speed Buggy," through "Starsky and Hutch" and the "Dukes of Hazzard," and ending with Burt Reynolds in the *Smokey and the Bandit* movies, we were told that speed was cool. Few boys learning to drive in the Seventies didn't try to pull a "Hutch," i.e., jump into the passenger side door while the car was moving, or play "Bandit" by hiding between 18-wheelers to elude state troopers on the highway.

The speed fantasy was never completely satisfying, though. No matter how fast we drove or how hard we pretended, Sally Field or Daisy Duke never showed up in the passenger seat and the truck filled with cold beer was never behind us when we stopped the speeding car. Just Dad or Smokey.

25. Driving Role Models that Let Us Down

Next thing we knew, Starsky and Hutch split up and Hutch became some wimpy guy named David Soul who sang songs our mothers liked. Brutal.

---

13 More Seventies Movies We Thought We Should Mention

13. *The Summer of '42*
12. *Midnight Express*
11. *Thank God It's Friday!*
10. *Superfly*
 9. *Walking Tall*
 8. *Mahogany*
 7. *All the President's Men*
 6. *The Sting*
 5. *That's Entertainment*
 4. *Rocky*
 3. *Butch Cassidy and the Sundance Kid*
 2. *Network*
 1. *Shampoo*

26. Cher's Navel

There it was, every week, before our eyes on the 19-inch color TV screen, elegantly surrounded by Bob Mackie costume fabric, calling out for all to behold. Its hypnotic power has never been truly understood. Its effect on American society has been dramatic.

Cher's navel truly screwed up our generation:

1. The attention span of America has been seriously impaired. Most people can't pay attention long enough to read a newspaper. Why? The psychological root of this phenomenon has been traced back to Wednesday nights at 8 P.M. We stared at Cher's navel while Sonny was trying to tell jokes.
2. We sweat with stairmaster, lifecycle, step aerobics, and cross training—the fitness craze is firmly embedded in our American lifestyle. Why? The weekly worship of Cher's navel. It's what we all aspired to, what obsessed our collective subconscious. We exercise as a continuance of this aspiration and to work down years of pent-up pre-teen and teenage sexual tension.
3. Cher's navel single-handedly opened the door for Madonna and her domination of pop music during the Eighties and Nineties.
4. "Orange Juice: it's not just for breakfast anymore." The entire resurgence of fruit juice consumption has been linked to our deep-rooted national navel obsession.

Fear for the Nineties: Butt tattoo craze.

27. Seventies Couples

Good luck matching these Seventies couples. Some are stage couples and some, frighteningly enough, are real couples. The answers, with some explanations, follow.

1.	Rocky Balboa	a.	Dinah Shore & Sally Field
2.	Lee Majors	b.	Barbra Streisand
3.	Sonny	c.	Linda Lovelace
4.	Fred Sanford	d.	Annie Hall
5.	Mike "Meathead" Stivic	e.	Mrs. C.
6.	Archie Bunker	f.	Geraldine Jones
7.	Oliver Barrett	g.	Bianca
8.	Brad	h.	Linda
9.	Mork	i.	Diana Hyland
10.	Mr. C.	j.	Janet
11.	Mike Brady	k.	Farrah Fawcett
12.	George Jefferson	l.	Carol
13.	Mary Hartman	m.	Angels
14.	Tony Orlando	n.	Toni Tennille
15.	Ken	o.	Nancy Spungen
16.	Sam	p.	Mary Hartman
17.	Steve Austin	q.	Yoko Ono
18.	Governor Jerry Brown	r.	Yo Adriene
19.	John Lennon	s.	& Cher
20.	Hugh Hefner	t.	Jenny Cavilleri
21.	Kris Kristofferson	u.	Barbi Benton
22.	Burt Reynolds	v.	Telma Hopkins and Joyce Vincent
23.	Reuben Kinkaid	w.	Edith
24.	John Travolta	x.	Barbie
25.	Chuck Traynor	y.	Jaime Sommers
26.	Alvie	z.	Alice
27.	David Birney	aa.	Shirley Partridge

28. Daryl Dragon	bb. Mindy McConnell
29. James Taylor	cc. Elizabeth
30. Paul McCartney	dd. Carly Simon
31. Mick Jagger	ee. Meredith Baxter
32. Hot Lips Houlihan	ff. Frank Burns
33. Sid Vicious	gg. Linda Ronstadt
34. Charlie Townsend	hh. Gloria
35. Flip Wilson	ii. Louise

answers: 1(r) Rocky Balboa and Yo Adriene. 2(k) Lee Majors and Farrah Fawcett (before Farrah became hyphenated). 3(s) Sonny and Cher (there is some hope for you if you missed this one). 4(cc) Fred Sanford and Elizabeth (his dead TV wife). 5(hh) Mike "Meat Head" Stivic and Gloria. 6(w) Archie Bunker and Edith. 7(t) Oliver Barrett and Jenny Cavilleri (the *Love Story* that made us all weep). 8(j) Brad and "Damn it! Janet!" from *Rocky Horror*. 9(bb) Mork and Mindy McConnell. (Did you ever wonder what their children would look like?) 10(e) Mr. and Mrs. C. 11(l) Mike and Carol Brady. (Did you ever wonder what birth control method they used to keep from having another little Brady?) 12(ii) George and Louise Jefferson. 13(p) Mary Hartman, Mary Hartman (Fernwood was a pretty funky town). 14(v) Tony Orlando, Telma Hopkins and Joyce Vincent, better known as Dawn. (It was fun fantasizing about the possibilities: *"Come here babies . . . Tie a yellow ribbon round this ole oak tree."*) 15(x) Ken and Barbie. 16(z) Sam the butcher and Alice. 17(y) The bionic couple. 18(gg) Governor Jerry Brown and Linda Ronstadt. (You almost forgot about this one, huh?) 19(q) John Lennon and Yoko Ono. (You wished you could forget her.) 20(u) Hugh Hefner and Barbi Benton. 21(b) Kris Kristofferson and Barbra Streisand. 22(a) Burt Reynolds and Dinah Shore & Sally Field. (No. Not at the same time. Gutter minds.) 23(aa) Reuben Kinkaid and Shirley Partridge. (Did they or didn't they? Only Danny knows.) 24(i) John Travolta and Diana Hyland. 25(c) Chuck Traynor and Linda Lovelace (the "Deep Throat" husband-and-wife team). 26(d) Alvie and Annie Hall. 27(ee) David Birney and Meredith Baxter. 28(n) Captain & Tennille (the muskrat lovers). 29(dd) James Taylor and Carly Simon. 30(h) Paul and Linda McCartney. 31(g) Mick and Bianca Jagger. 32(ff) Hot Lips Houlihan and Frank Burns (Hawkeye Pierce insisted that Frank be placed in the female column). 33(o) Sid Vicious and Nancy Spungen (his groupie girlfriend he had murdered). 34(m) Charlie and his Angels. (Charlie is either the stupidest or the kinkiest guy in the Seventies! Would you use an intercom to communicate with these Angels?) 35(f) Flip Wilson and Geraldine Jones. (This couple truly screwed up the twentysomething generation!)

28. KISS

Dear Gene, Ace, Peter and Paul,

On the afternoon of my 13th birthday in 1977, I ran out and ravenously purchased "Kiss—Alive," "KISS—Rock & Roll Over" and "KISS—Destroyer." I was the last kid on the block to acquire these fundamental prizes for my record collection. I voraciously tore off the shrink wrap, and immediately transferred the awesome "Rock & Roll Over" KISS stickers to my denim notebook cover. I flipped open "KISS—Alive" and read the personal notes from you, wishing I could be half as cool as the two dudes

pictured at your concert on the back album cover. After listening religiously for over four hours and carefully placing my treasures alphabetically in my record crate, I emerged from my room in a rock 'n roll daze. I beamed with teenage pride, bragging about my purchase and showing off my stickers the next day at school . . .

On the afternoon of my 30th birthday this year, I found myself flipping through the CD rack at Tower Records, and there, to my complete dismay, between Carol King and Led Zeppelin, was a new nineties KISS Album. I froze and screamed "Why? Why? Why?" I had not touched my KISS albums since that one-day obsession with your group almost two decades ago, and this flashback at the CD rack was too much to handle. I tore home from Tower, in search of an answer. In a deja vu haze, I dusted off "KISS—Destroyer," cleaned the vinyl with my oak-handled disk washer, turned the stereo to eleven and reexperienced side one's "Detroit Rock City". . .

I sit here, dazed and confused by my past teenage mentality and unorthodox present behavior. What had I been thinking? What warped force of nature possessed me to spend my sacred birthday money on such senseless terror so many years ago? Was it the same force that struck me today in Tower Records and forced me to relive the pain? I am scared and disoriented. Please help me.

Dear Fan,

The burning tongue spits fire and smoke through the black night of your cloudy room. Aaaaughh, spit, snort, lick, slurp, rock-on, rock-on, rock-on. The fierce beast of hell torments the love monster and cries his songs of pain. Sleep deep gentle snake, sleep deep.

29. Where Old Stars Go to Die

The environmentalism of the Seventies taught us that you don't throw things away, you recycle them. And two

Welcome to Fantasy Island, whoever you are!

TV shows cleverly came up with a way to apply this principle of conservation to another valuable resource: has-been actors.

What do you do with the ex-stars of "Bridget Loves Bernie"? Let them be guest stars on "The Love Boat." What ever happened to Arte Johnson? Let's cast him in this week's "Fantasy Island."

Yes, "The Love Boat" and "Fantasy Island" were more than inane comedy/drama series, they were a way to keep countless small names off the unemployment lines. Each week, these shows could utilize up to a dozen such actors, which far exceeded the capacity of the "To Tell the Truth" panel of the Sixties.

And unlike talk shows and game shows, this was real *acting*. I'm sure a guest spot on one of these two programs would make John Davidson's year ("Oh, of course, in 1977 I was busy shooting a TV show . . .").

The cancellation of these shows meant hardship for these marginal celebrities, most of them have been forced into dinner theater, their ranks now augmented by Ricardo Montalban, Gavin MacLeod and Lauren Tewes. Perhaps, someday, they will be rescued by that most forgiving patron saint of TV actors: *syndication*.

30. Garry Marshall

Garry Marshall tried to make the Seventies a little more bearable by showing us life in saner, happier times. We saw how cool it was to live in the Fifties with characters like Fonzie, Chachi, Pinky and Leather Tuscadero in "Happy Days." Even Potsie, Ralph and Richie Cunningham were cooler than we were in the Seventies. Laverne and Shirley, Lenny and Squiggy: eccentric, certainly, but they had undeniable style. And of course, Mork from Ork was the ultimate unconventionalist, whose interplanetary "Na-nu, Na-nu" took us by storm. Come to think of it, I'm not sure these shows did make us feel any better . . . all these characters and places were a lot better off than we were in the Seventies. We were left wishing we were somebody we weren't, in a place that probably didn't exist. But, hey, things are much the same with today's TV shows: "Beverly Hills 90210," "Melrose Place" and "Baywatch" show us worlds that are certainly far from our own. Are there really people like Brandon and Dylan on our planet? One hopes not. On Ork, perhaps.

13 Things that Made a Girl Really Cool

13. Braided hair on really special occasions (like a date to The Polka Dot Crustless Pizza Parlor).
12. Earth shoes, clogs, or five-inch heels on platform shoes.
11. Farrah flip hair.
10. Bracelets: macrame, P.O.W., M.I.A., or leather.
 9. Smoking.
 8. Being up on "General Hospital."
 7. Painted toenails or black bras.
 6. Yellow comb sticking out of Gloria Vanderbilt jeans back pocket.
 5. Puka shell necklace.
 4. Incredible assortment of Bonne Belle Lip Smackers.
 3. Robin's egg blue eye shadow.
 2. French kissing with Bubble Yum in mouth.
 1. Breasts.

Killer bee

31. Great Catastrophes of the Seventies

Killer Bees. They were said to be heading north on their migratory path from the deepest jungles of Mexico. They were said to be as big as birds and as poisonous as vipers. They were said to be as vicious as piranhas as they swarm-attacked innocent children. They were said to be invading the continent at any time. They must have taken a wrong turn. Talk about the *bee* who cried wolf.

Legionnaires Disease. The bacteria that infected a large number of American Legion officials at a convention during the summer of 1976 in Philadelphia was believed to have been spread through the hotel's central air conditioning ducts. This bizarre catastrophe prompted us to ask the question central to our own mortality: Is it better to risk an unusual disease or melt in Philadelphia's summer heat? The best answer: avoid Philadelphia altogether.

Swine Flu. Anyone warped enough to get intimate with pigs deserves what they get.

Falling of Skylab. This is the classic Seventies catastrophe. Man builds a heavy, sharp metal object and throws it in the air. Man forgets that it will fall back down on his head.

32. Riggs' Pigs

The National Organization of Women, the Equal Rights Amendment, *Roe vs. Wade*, Shirley Chisholm running for president, Gloria Steinem creating *Ms.* magazine, Bella Abzug defying the fashion industry with her hats . . . The boys in elementary school were clueless about these ground-breaking events and people in the early Seventies. While the boys had their suspicions that something was up when they eavesdropped on Mom singing Helen Reddy's "I Am Woman" or when big sister proclaimed her rights by burning her bra and "going natural," the whole women's movement "thing" left their asphalt playgrounds unaffected until one fateful day.

September 21, 1973. The morning after Billy Jean King beat Bobby Riggs (the prototypic male chauvinist pig) in straight sets on the tennis court. It was the boys'

PE teacher who delivered the news. Coach "Big Butt" Budd pulled the boys aside and spoke with a nervous, hushed voice, "Little men, I think we have a problem . . ."

It was a tragic day for the boys who had grown used to the mutually agreed upon segregated playgrounds, where the boys played on one side and the girls on the other. Billy Jean changed all of that. A girl actually beat a boy! The "Battle of the Sexes" and Women's Lib finally hit the schoolyard. From that moment on, girls invaded every sacred sport—no sport was safe.

No longer did the boys move in from the outfield when the girls were at the plate waiting to kick the rubber ball or hit the softball on the stick, for fear that the ball would fly over the boys' heads. No longer did the boys taunt the girls on the opposing dodgeball team by dancing inches from the dividing line, for fear that a stinging ball would hit them south of the equator. There was always the chance that the "Curse of Bobby Riggs" could strike. Anywhere. Anytime.

33. The New York City Marathon

Somehow in the late Seventies, during the height of the running craze, the sweaty but tightknit circle of marathoners expanded to include middle-aged Wall Street lawyers from the Upper East Side.

Ten thousand "runners" limp and hobble by a group of two million spectators that stretch themselves along the twenty-six-mile course and cheer in sadistic glee. Not unlike the running of the bulls at the Festival of San Fermine in Pamplona, Spain, this crowd waits for the unlucky runner who will trip and fall beneath the trampling hoofs of some butcher from Brooklyn who is doing this "because if I finish, by wife promises to never say the word 'diet' again."

However, most New Yorkers run in the marathon because it is a great way to be seen by two million people in Manhattan. It also offers some of the cheapest adver-

A long way to the finish line

tising rates around. Every year the Verrazano Narrows Bridge is carpeted with a motley swarm of two-legged billboards exclaiming everything from "Buy Haim's Kosher" to "If you think this *race* is long, call 555–1742 for a marathon . . . of love."

34. Feminine Footwear

The din of the bulls' hooves running the streets of Pamplona was equalled only by the racket produced by a gaggle of adolescent girls clomping down a linoleum-lined hallway in clogs. Clogs were trendy. Clogs were European. But most importantly, clogs were easily removed to expose the true bane of Seventies foot apparel: the toe sock.

Like little knit gloves for the feet, a toe sock's prestige was determined by the different colors of each toe "slot." The proud wearer of the toe socks that spanned the spectrum of the color wheel from left-foot-little-toe to right-foot-little-toe almost invariably won front mirror space in the girls' lavatory and free use of anyone's lip gloss. The toe sock craze peaked with the introduction of numbered toes (in English, Spanish, and French for

Platform shoes

educational purposes) and the socks that offered cute toe names embroidered onto each toe "casing."

Mercifully, the age of the toe sock ended when mood rings forced us to refocus attention on some of our more presentable—and accessible—digits.

Oh yes, they call him the streak

35. Streaking

Question: What is more embarrassing than wagging your genitals in front of a live television audience?

Answer: Doing it on purpose.

Seventies frivolity reached its peak in April 1974, when Robert Opel streaked behind David Niven during the Academy Award ceremonies.

The streaker must feel a unique sense of freedom: running loose, unencumbered by the trappings of modern day vanity, letting the wind explore new nooks and crannies, knowing that at any time three large men might tackle and shackle him and arrest him for indecent exposure.

If I were arrested for streaking, I would prefer not to be charged with indecent exposure. Something like impressive exposure or inspiring exposure would be nicer.

36. Puma Clydes

Next to today's Pump and Air technologies, the Puma Clyde seems prehistoric. But in the mid-Seventies, Clydes were the coolest kicks in the cave. If you didn't have those two heavy, thick pieces of suede draped over your feet you sure weren't going to be picked first on the kickball team. Many shoe companies tried to imitate the Clyde but always failed because Clyde's had one characteristic that couldn't be copied: after one day of normal wear they smelled like something had crawled up in the toe and died.

37. Masterpiece

"How much will you bid for this Engelbert Humperdinck?" Brenda called out to the three other girls in her bedroom, trying to start an auction.

"Nothing. It's probably a forgery," responded one of the girls with a snicker.

"Come on, it could be worth millions," Brenda urged, trying desperately to rid herself of the forgery.

"Auction your Leif Garrett. I'd start the bidding at $500,000. He's such a hunk."

Despondent, Brenda dropped her Humperdinck and put her Leif up for auction. Twenty seconds later she received $1,000,000.

Brenda and her friends were playing *their* version of the Parker Brothers game Masterpiece. Instead of going around the board and collecting Rembrandt, Renoir, and Van Gogh masterpieces, they replaced the paintings with pictures of people like Scott Baio, Erik Estrada, and Parker Stevenson. This made the game more interesting and personal. After all, one person's Humperdinck is another's Hardy Boy.

38. Ninth-Grade Romance

Prologue

"I know he likes you," Kathleen giggled, twirling the stringy elastic mass of Bubble Yum around her index finger.

"Quit it," hushed Carol, trying to tame a long strand of her blond hair that had fallen out of place.

The pair had been best friends since elementary school. They had shared the pleasures of The Barbie Game, sang Cher songs on the Ronco Mr. Music II, and read the same copies of Judy Blume novels. They both thought Shaun Cassidy was the dreamiest Hardy Boy and that Kate Jackson was the coolest Angel, despite their own matching manes of Farrah "flip" hair. Now it was ninth grade, and their class ruled the junior high school. An atmosphere of excitement and anticipation filled the locker-lined halls, as the first week of classes came to a close. Carol and Kathleen walked with the assuredness of fashion models as they finally emerged from the second-floor girls' bathroom.

"Monday afternoon, I'm telling you, at your locker," Kathleen predicted. The whole school had heard the rumor that Jim was going to ask Carol out. The two had flirted all summer as their "gang" hung out at the town park. Jim had shown off his mastery of the high dive which sparked Carol's sense of adventure. Carol sported her carefully chosen bikini, stirring youthful affection in Jim's heart and teenage passion in his swim trunks. Needless to say, Jim had spent most of the summer tanning his back.

Everybody knew that the two were destined for each other; it was now only a matter of time. Carol and Kathleen turned the corner to head down the science corridor.

"Hello, ladies," It was Chris, Jim's best friend. "K.T., I need to talk to you."

This was Kathleen's nickname, used only by her closest friends and confidants. K.T. smiled knowingly and made mischievous eye contact with Carol. She and Chris were responsible for romantic logistics, motivation, and communication between their respective best friends. The two shuffled quickly into the earth science classroom to complete preparation for the upcoming summit meeting. Carol leaned back against a locker, heart racing, impatiently waiting.

The Boys

Joel, Chris, Elliot, and Brian huddled quietly in the woodland clearing. It was almost 10:00, and the night had grown unusually cold. Brian sipped carefully on the solitary Schlitz beer he had lifted from the refrigerator while his father's back was turned. Elliot dangled a cigarette from his lower lip, squinting as the smoke curled upward into his eyes. Chris glanced nervously, also smoking a cigarette, hoping that the others couldn't tell that he wasn't inhaling.

After a long pause, Joel finally broke the silence: "So, when's he going to ask her?"

Chris responded, "Monday afternoon, at her locker, after the final bell."

"Well, we know what Jimmy'll be doing Monday night!" Joel replied. His friends echoed the sentiment with a rousing chorus of grunting, moaning, and smooching noises.

Just then, Jim emerged through the bushes that surrounded their secret recreational hideaway. The taunting and teasing sounds crescendoed to a peak, with hooting, clapping, whistling, and various obscene hand gestures.

"Yeah, right." Jim attempted a comeback, slightly embarrassed but still glowing with anticipation. His friends persisted with their loud, malicious, yet truly envious harassment.

A siren was heard off in the distance. The boys froze. It grew louder.

"C'mon!" shouted Brian as he and the others took off, sprinting through the suburban forest.

The clearing had never been found by the town police, and thanks to teenage ingenuity and secret trails marked by their predecessors, the boys were able to uphold this tradition. Joel, Chris, Brian and Elliot reveled in their escape, formulating the tale that would become folklore throughout the junior high school. Although Jim shared their excitement, he couldn't stop thinking about Carol and the foreboding moment that rapidly approached.

The Girls

A tense hush blanketed the candle-lit eeriness of Carol's bedroom. Stephanie, Lisa, Hope, and Gail huddled around the Ouija board, their hands piled nervously on the magical moving piece. Carol closed her eyes tightly and whispered, "Will he ask me? Will he ask me?" She placed her palms on top of the others' and called upon the forces of nature.

The girls clung closely together as they committed to their supernatural journey. K.T. was sprawled on the bed, away from the others, toying with the "Magic 8-Ball." Spooky stuff made her uncomfortable, so she kept her distance. She hoped the time would pass quickly, looking forward to the crank phone calls and "truth or dare" game that were next on the slumber party agenda.

"Will he ask me?" Carol repeated, softly, slowly. The heap of female hands began to drift across the Ouija board. "Will he ask me?" Another inch closer, guided only by unknown omniscient energy. "Will he ask me?" Closer. "Will he ask me?" Closer. "Will he . . ."

"Yes! He's going to ask you out!" shouted K.T. from the bed, breaking the spiritual spell.

"Hey!" shouted the girls, frustrated by Kathleen's disbelief and disrespect.

"Wait, look!" interrupted Lisa.

Every eye in the room became riveted on the Ouija Board. The forces of nature had revealed the answer all had hoped for.

"I told you so," muttered K.T. as she adjusted her position on the bed. Without warning, the Magic 8-Ball fell from her hands and landed in front of Carol on the floor. When she picked it up, her eyes widened, for it too revealed the answer "YES."

The Main Event

Every eye in the hallway was focused on Jim as he approached Carol at her locker. Carol pretended to be unaware, inspecting her hair in the locker door compact mirror; inside, however, she was shaking with anticipation. Jim stepped up. The hallway hushed.

"Hi," said Jim.

"Hi," said Carol.

"Will you go out with me?" asked Jim.

"Okay," answered Carol.

"Great," said Jim, "see ya later."

"Great," said Carol, "okay."

With that, it was official.

The Relationship

For almost three weeks, Carol and Jim were a hot item. They held hands at the movies and sat next to each other on the bus. They kissed for an extra long time during Spin-the-Bottle and got jealous when it was someone else's turn to cut in. They rode double on Jim's bike. They danced together twice during the Friday night disco party, retreating quickly to opposite sides of the room once the music stopped. They thought about going to second base, but chickened out. By early October, it seemed that the flame was dwindling; that the magic was gone.

The Break-Up

Every eye in the hallway was focused on Carol as she approached Jim at his locker. Jim pretended to be unaware, foraging through the pockets of his jean jacket; inside, however, he was shaking with anticipation. Carol stepped up. The hallway hushed.

"Hi," said Carol.

"Hi," said Jim.

"You wanna break up?" asked Carol.

"Okay," answered Jim.

"Great," said Carol, "see ya later."

"Great," said Jim, "okay."

With that, it was official.

Epilogue

"I know he likes you," Kathleen giggled, twirling the stringy elastic mass of Bubble Yum around her index finger.

"Quit it," hushed Carol, trying to tame a long strand of her blond hair that had fallen out of place.

The whole school had heard the rumor that Brian was going to ask Carol out. Everybody knew that the two were destined for each other; it was now only a matter of time . . .

39. . . . and a Partridge in a Pear Tree

Leader: "Okay now, go ahead. Don't be afraid."

Margaret: "Hello, My name is Margaret, and I have a Partridge Family problem."

Group: "Hello, Margaret."

Margaret: "Ummm . . . I had my 'Sound Magazine' LP bronzed last week in honor of Reuben Kinkaid's birthday."

Applause

Leader: "Very good, Margaret! Now, who's next?"

Nathan: "My name is Nathan. I love Danny Bonaduce's Chicago radio show. I love it so much. It's all I listen to." *Applause*

Karen: "My name is Karen, and I thought David Cassidy's Broadway performance in *Blood Brothers* was brilliant, truly brilliant. It was breathtaking to see him on stage again. *Cats? Les Mis?* What's next?" *Applause*

Debbi: "My name is Debbi, and I just painted my bus and put a sign on the back saying, 'Caution. Nervous Mother Driving'." *Applause*

Jules: "I'm Jules and I still don't understand why Chris was first played by Jeremy Gelbwaks and then switched to Brian Forster. I mean, come on. Two different people? I'm so confused." *Applause*

Phoebe: "Hi, I'm Phoebe, and I still cry every Thursday night since 'L.A. Law' was canceled." *Applause*

Danny: "I woke up in love this morning, I woke up in love this morning!"

Tracy: "Hi, I'm Tracy."

Leader: "Thank you for all of your comments. Now it's time to close the meeting with our happy song."

Applause

Tracy: "But, I really *am* Tracy. Look, here's my tambourine . . ."

Leader: "Everyone, let's all sing 'Come On, Get Happy!' Ready . . ."

40. Dieting

It was only natural that during a decade of skin-tight hip-huggers and exposed midriffs, dieting came of age. The Seventies brought a wealth of new products and gimmicks that ensured us of dieting fads with the same regularity as new clothes and hair styles.

Sure, cyclamates were out, but they were soon replaced by saccharin in our Tab and Diet Rite and No-Cal

Soda. God knows what chemical atrocities went into making Slenderella jelly, Metrecal, Alba and Alba 77 (the sugar-free milk-shake substitute), but we consumed them all. And we had plenty of help and advice, from Stillman's water diet (drink eight to ten glasses of water a day in *addition* to what you already eat and drink) to the Elton John plan (weight loss through tennis) to *Count Your Carbohydrates!* (which claimed that calories were unimportant as long as you kept your carbohydrate count low; under this preposterous regimen, my mother and I gorged ourselves on pork rinds and cream cheese for weeks and *actually believed* we would lose weight).

We devoured each new diet with the same enthusiasm we had for Hostess snack cakes. But, alas, the weight always seemed to reappear, driving us back to our loose-fitting polyester smocks and granny dresses. Our only consolation was this: If history indeed repeats itself, then before too long the Victorian standards of beauty will be back, when plump women were considered the very height of feminine perfection. When this happens, we thought to ourselves, we'll be ready.

41. Super Elastic Bubble Plastic

This children's toy could be used in two ways:

1. Squeeze a small amount of the plastic out of the tube, roll it in a ball, place it at the end of the little straw, and blow it up into a colorful, non-toxic balloon.
2. Squeeze it all out into the bathroom sink, lock the door, put a towel over your head and breathe

Out-of-body experience with super elastic bubble plastic

deeply. Rub the remaining plastic into your mother's rug and your sister's hair.

42. Debby Boone

"You Light Up My Life" won a Grammy Award in 1977 and went on to become *Billboard's* Number One Song of the Entire Decade.

What were we thinking?

43. Bulbous Cars

What happened to sleek engineering in the Seventies? The prototype for the Ford Pinto was designed one Sunday morning out of a stack of pancakes and four butter balls. The AMC Pacer was worse. Many thought it looked as good on the road as it did in the living room filled with water and tropical fish. Then AMC upholstered the interior of its Gremlin with blue jean denim. Unbelievable.

VW's The Thing is appropriately named. When I was a kid my mother would assemble all the month-old leftovers, bake them at 900°F, and call it a "casserole." We called it "The Thing." Some German design engineer with a sense of humor looked around the factory floor, saw all the scrap metal, thought of my mother's casserole, and put the leftover metal to good use. Ugly, but very nutritious.

44. Cars Built for Safety

The Ford Pinto helped clear the road of pesky tail-gaters, the same way landmines help promote quick weight loss.

Drivers of wood-paneled station wagons always avoided hazardous driving because every morning they opened their garage door to see a car made out of wood and then quickly remembered what happened to the Three Little Pigs.

---

13 Things Our Parents Believed Screwed Us Up

13. Marijuana.
12. Lamaze childbirthing.
11. Rod Stewart's "Do Ya Think I'm Sexy?" and Donna Summer's "Love to Love You Baby."
10. All those boys in loud cars.
 9. TV remote control.
 8. Black light posters.
 7. Ouija board.
 6. New math.
 5. Artificial sweeteners.
 4. The Sweathogs.
 3. Sex education.
 2. Subliminal messages.
 1. Right turn on red.

45. Little House on the Prairie

"Oh, to have a Dad like Charles Ingalls, a caring blind sister like Mary, and a splendid general store in town with a great candy counter. I wish I was Laura, running down the hill on a beautiful spring day, wearing those wonderful dresses and bonnets. What a warm, happy world she lives in! Wouldn't it be great?!"

"Shut up and move! We're not watching 'Little House on the *Fairy*,' no way!"

Big brothers often won the battle. Ten-year-old little sisters were pushed aside left only to dream and plot their revenge.

Big brothers grew up to become boyfriends and husbands. Little sisters grew up to become girlfriends and wives who drag their boyfriends and husbands to see movies like *Sleepless in Seattle* and *Thelma & Louise*. If you watch closely in the dark of movie theaters, you can see women making eye contact and nodding knowingly— the "Prairie Pact" is being upheld. As men watch Meg Ryan weep on the top of the Empire State Building, they humbly acknowledge that these former ten-year-old sisters have truly triumphed.

46. Brave New Salty Snack

Aldous Huxley would have been proud when a consumer goods company created Pringles—the "brave new world" of salty snacks.

"Everyone is created equal. The idea is so American that it's in the Constitution!" mused some marketing executive in charge of future products when he or she developed the idea of cloning potato chips in the image of the perfect chip. Same shape, same subtle aerodynamic curve, same bland flavor that would make even the stalest communion wafer blush.

And if this cloning idea sells, why not make M&M's all the same color? Donuts all the same shape (what the hell is a cruller)? Fruit Loops all the same flavor? Condoms all the same size?

We could program people from birth to take certain jobs and make their world so perfect that no individual decisions would ever need to be made again. All of this sprung from the birth of a simple consumer product . . . how wonderfully American.

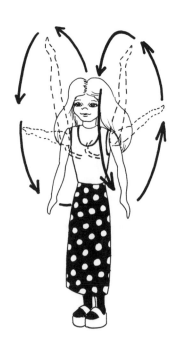

Growing-up Skipper in action

47. Growing Up Skipper

If only my breast development at the age of eleven were that simple.

When I added Skipper, Barbie's younger sister, to my collection of dolls, she was a pirate's dream—a sunken chest. But that was before I started twisting her arms around and around—then bazooom! Blossoming into a teenager, she grew nearly an inch taller, her hips slimmed and some boobs developed. No more training bras for her! Ken and Todd were in love with Skipper. Barbie, Midge, and Christie were so jealous.

With Skipper to inspire me, I twisted my arms throughout the day and into the night hoping to become a woman. I'd brush my teeth with one hand and twist with the other. I'd twist with both arms flailing on the way to the school bus. I'd twist little twists in the stall of the girls' lavatory. I'd twist before going to bed. I twisted so much my little sister thought I was trying to fly, but she left me alone when I told her I was practicing the backstroke.

Months later, I was the same height and my breasts were . . . *deflating!* There was no doubt about it. From every angle in the full-length mirror I could see that they were getting smaller. I panicked. It was so easy for Skipper. What had gone wrong for me? Was I doing it all wrong?

After one week of intense worry, I figured out that my shoulders and arm muscles had gotten much larger, making my breasts look smaller.

How stupid of me! I've been twisting my arms in the wrong direction!

48. Animal House

I actually began to curse National Lampoon's *Animal House* during the summer of 1978. Yes, it's a cinematic classic that gave birth to the zany humor of John Landis, Ivan Reitman, Harold Ramis, and their powerhouse genre of "Saturday Night Live" inspired movies (*Caddyshack, Stripes, Trading Places, Ghostbusters*). Yes, it had important educational implications, motivating many of America's less studious teenagers to consider college for the first time. Yes, I saw it three times in the theater. But by late-1978, the aftermath of *Animal House* had become overwhelming. My fifteen-year-old hormones had a very difficult time adjusting to the endless wave of toga parties that broke out after the movie's success. For months and months, the only things that separated tenth grade men from tenth grade women were loosely wrapped, white sheets and carefully placed safety pins. Every Friday and Saturday night, suburban households filled with scantily clad and sweaty Romans with raging libidos. We danced to the wild sounds of Otis Day and the Knights, sang "Shout" and fell to the ground in convulsions like Bluto. No Mayor's daughter or jar of mustard was safe. I was permanently flushed and out of breath by the end of my sophomore year. My academic performance slipped along with my morals. I solidly blame John Landis for this early foray into sexual frustration, and at the same time thank him wholeheartedly for my few sacred occasions of toga inspired promiscuity.

49. Presidential Physical Fitness

Patches were cool. Being a jock was cooler. Presidential Physical Fitness patches combined the two to become the "absolute coolest."

To win a presidential patch, the hopeful young contender had to endure a program of pulling-up, sitting-up,

pushing-up, running-up, and jumping-up without throwing-up.

The standards were very high and only a few proud warriors boasted a presidential patch on their arm. Until the day that Rocco "Fingers" Durham, the baddest dude in the sixth grade, "found" a whole box of the patches in the coach's office. Word spread quickly. Ultimate coolness was suddenly possible—if you could pay the price.

Gallons worth of milk money found its way into Rocco's pocket until the coach noticed an unusually high number of people strutting the halls displaying the patch of ultimate coolness. He quickly surmised what had happened and called the entire sixth grade into the gym for a special meeting. There he announced that the school had established an "extra special" fitness award, "The Coach's Award," that signified an even higher level of coolness.

Market prices tumbled, Rocco retired to the seventh grade where he remained throughout most of his adolescent years, and we were all afforded our first exposure to currency devaluation.

50. Digital Watches

What better way to top off the man-made splendor of polyester clothing than with the latest in time-keeping technology, the digital watch? In the Seventies, they perfected something called the "LED," which stood for "Light-Emitting Diode." Whatever it was, it made possible watches that would light up in red digits to tell you the time. This not only enabled us to wear digital watches on our arms, but permitted us to demonstrate our superior knowledge by explaining to our friends what

"LED" stood for. It was great: fashion and technology merged into one. Never mind that you needed to push the button to see what time it was. Never mind that you couldn't see the numbers in the daylight. Never mind the fact that there was nothing wrong with the *old* watches.

Digital watches burst into my life during junior high school, and I simply had to have one. They were new. They were cool. Mom and Dad thought they were stupid, which made them all the more desirable. Then one day during a handball game I "accidentally" scratched my old watch beyond all redemption. No two ways about it, I needed a new timepiece.

Several weeks of pleading and bargaining finally led to victory; I soon found myself in the local catalog showroom store with Mom at my side, staring longingly into the watch case. "Nothing over $50," she cautioned.

I selected a stunning digital masterpiece with a black metal band. It was manufactured by some Japanese company I'd never heard of, which worried Mom, but didn't faze me. I knew this watch was the coolest. Just wait till they saw it flashing out on the handball court!

Of course, Mom was right and I was wrong. The few weeks of being cool were hardly worth having to constantly push the damned button and being unable to see what time it was in daylight. And the unknown Japanese company was apparently a fly-by-night enterprise: three months later, my watch died a sudden, painless death during chemistry class. It was a long time before I trusted technology again.

51. The Blight of AM Radio

For a long time, AM was it. Not much of a choice. The FM band was reserved for esoteric, progressive programming. AM liked top-40 hits that were under three minutes. FM got everything else: weird college DJs and religious talk shows.

Then came Don McLean. "American Pie" was very long and very popular. The AM program directors didn't know what to do. This song was triple the normal length but people liked it. AM stations played "American Pie" and other musicians realized that they no longer had to be mainstream and write three minute songs about love and daisies. Plus their music sounded better on FM. The AM stations were facing a revolution in song length and content and they just couldn't handle it. FM picked up the slack and took over.

George Carlin's "Seven Things You Can't Say" were said on FM. Now AM has the religious talk shows. *Hah!*

52. Magic

Believe it or not, Doug Henning was cool. Yes, that's right, a long-haired, buck-toothed, jumpsuit-sporting, platform-shoed character took the nation by storm. He had television specials and even a Broadway show created in his image. His success came quickly and powerfully through sleight-of-hand and flashy illusion. We praised Doug and emulated his talent, for he, unlike our meager mortal selves, was a magician.

We eagerly read the magic catalogues, spending our scarce allowance to order the latest tricks. I had the "rope illusion package," the "Chinese metal rings" and "the finger chopper" (an extremely popular, sibling torture device). Debbie, my next door neighbor, would come over and help me stage magic shows for my very patient and humoring family. Magic was more than a hobby, it was a living force that held the key to pre-teen popularity and some warped form of social status. Mastering this force meant total success in life and complete happiness.

Thus, we lived unsuccessfully and unhappily, struggling to make sense of poorly illustrated instructions that came with our cheap, made-in-Taiwan "magic" devices. Once or twice, we would get a trick right, feeling that sudden burst of elation, but the momentous event occurred while alone in our rooms with no one to bear witness to the feat. Hah! Score another point for Doug Henning! He made it look so easy—every time—with that smug smile and goofy laugh, showing off his divine talent to the struggling masses who watched him amidst a tangled web of silk handkerchiefs, coins, and playing cards. We deeply thirsted for the gift of illusion, but soon gave up our quest in frustration, letting our dreams of success fade like the brown and yellow shades of the family-room carpet.

Today we sit, scarred by our failure, but perhaps also better prepared to face the REAL magic we encounter every day in the nineties: personal digital assistants that bounce messages from our pockets to points around the globe, fax machines that make documents materialize into our homes, offices and cars, virtual reality helmets that allow us to experience an alternate universe, microwave ovens that prepare banquets in seconds. We can take it all in stride, using these fabulous inventions without the slightest understanding of how they work. Unlike the mysterious linking rings, we can master these incredible feats with minimal practice by pressing a few buttons.

Doug Henning, you were good, but I think we've outdone you now. I never saw YOU defrost meat in five minutes flat.

53. Skateboards

When skateboards were outfitted with non-turning, squeaky metal wheels, they were a simple, harmless way to get to the corner store. The introduction of urethane wheels and high-tech trucks made them speeding transporters for death-defying adolescents. These improvements in technology made the skateboard more maneuverable, and therefore more menacing:

- Simple skitching (grabbing a car's rear bumper for a free ride) was replaced by the high-speed highway skitch.

- Boarding from side to side in the family bathtub became aerial acrobatics in a twenty-foot half-pipe.
- The traditional slalom became too easy so the fluorescent cones were replaced by senior citizens on walkers.

54. Cool Candles

At the age of twelve, by mistake or by some merciful act of God, BJ was invited to Tia's fourteenth birthday party. BJ, a barely known rider of bus #283, was asked to attend a party given by Tia, the most popular and beautiful debutante on the bus. This was his chance to become known—to make an impression. This occasion called for the perfect gift, and no expense could be spared. And there was only one place that could assure him of picking out that special something from among its wondrous wares: The Candle Shop.

The Candle Shop in the Oak Park Mall specialized in candles. Its shelves were strewn with every color and shape and scent; candles that looked like cats and smileys and elves and unicorns and basically anything else you'd want to own (or, perhaps, want to see burned). Candles were the perfect gift: personal and yet noncommittal. Extremely fashionable in the Seventies and yet timeless, since the favorite ice-cream-soda-shaped candle would be treasured long into adulthood. How could it not? Candles were attractive knickknacks that complemented any teenage decor, while at the same time they were useful—as a source of light and a means to create that special mood that only the aroma of molten wax could create. (Of course, no one ever actually used their candles, but they *could* have, and that's what counted.)

BJ spent a full half-hour perusing the flammable goods before he made his selection—the purple-and-white De-luxe Enchanted Castle. At $12.95, it was well worth the three-weeks allowance, and it was sure to delight Tia in a way that would assure his invitation to future social events.

Was he trying to buy friendships and popularity? Of course. But adolescence was a desperate time.

55. Star Wars

The original lyrics for *Star Wars* were discovered in John Williams' London townhouse in 1978 by Mr. Williams' housekeeper, Annette. Previously unpublished, the words were written by Cynthia Anderson, Mr. Williams' ambitious ten-year-old niece. Despite the fact that the lyrics were never used, this author finds Ms. Anderson's work both poetic and moving, to say the very least. (to be sung to the tune of *Star Wars*)

(main theme)
Star Wars, nothing but Star Wars, gotta love Star
    Wars, every night.
Star Wars, beautiful Star Wars, watch Luke
    Skywalker, put up a fight.

(middle section)
There's Hans . . . Solo, Princess Leia and Obi-Wan
Flying high . . . up above the planet
There's Chew . . . baka, R-2-D-2, C-3-P-O,
And Darth Vader with his awful, evil, friends.

(main theme)
Star Wars, come and see Star Wars, pay lots of
money, to uncle John.
Star Wars, time to see Star Wars, talk to your
mother, she'll come along.

(repeat and fade out)
Star Wars, nothing but Star Wars . . .

56. Seventies Music: Trying to Make Sense of it All

Professor Gibbson Cassidy, Ph.D.

A PUBLIC SERVICE FROM PROFESSOR GIBBSON CASSIDY, Ph.D.*

CHAPTER I: INTRODUCTION

"A song must have a particular sound and a particular feeling to fall into the infamous category of Seventies music. Simply being released between 1970 and 1980 is not, in itself, enough."

—*Dick Clark*

---

*Professor of Historic Discology.

"I never said that."

—*Dick Clark*

So, what exactly is "Seventies music"? There is no clear definition for this absurd force that has profoundly affected the course of American culture. Thousands of songs were released during the decade, by artists ranging from the Carpenters to Led Zeppelin, yet only a fraction of them can truly qualify as Seventies music. What characteristics set these songs apart, deeming them appropriate for "K-tel" albums and Studio 54 dance parties? What are the qualities that make these songs so ridiculous to remember, yet so impossible to forget?

For most people, Seventies music is instantly recognizable, in fact, most human beings have a profound physical reaction to the sounds of "Boogie Fever" and "Disco Inferno." When they hear the thumping bass line and the classic "wick-ah, wick-ah" of an electric guitar, their heads turn sideways, their eyes roll backward, and their mouths break out into embarrassed smiles. These effects occur as the brain floods with memories of blow-dried hair, leisure suits, halter tops, and bell bottoms.

However, it is important to remember that Seventies music is not defined by disco alone. The genre represents a diverse collection of sounds and styles that eludes any textbook definition. How does one accurately categorize "Love Will Keep Us Together" or "Afternoon Delight?" How does one classify artists like ABBA and the Bay City Rollers? Recognizing Seventies music can be a confusing psychological, physiological, and somewhat pathological experience.

To truly appreciate Seventies music and fully comprehend its effect on the twentysomething generation, we must attempt to adopt a working definition, a classification system that sifts through the decade and separates

"Stairway to Heaven" from "Shake Your Groove Thing." Once we successfully sort and categorize, it will be clear how warped our musical tastes and behavior really, truly were. We must strive to understand our past; these historical insights are the only weapons we have to help us confront the musical insanity we now face in the Nineties and to help protect against the ominous musical forces that lie ahead.

Professor Cassidy pays homage to the great Travolta

CHAPTER II: CLASSIFICATION

What Seventies Music Is Not

Any song that is frequently played on rock or pop radio stations of the Nineties is automatically disqualified from Seventies classification. Excluded are all "classic rock" tunes from musical super-groups like the Beatles, the Rolling Stones, Aerosmith, and the Who; songs by super-artists like Eric Clapton and Bruce Springsteen; Motown hits from artists like the Temptations and Stevie Wonder, and even punk offerings from groups like the Sex Pistols and The Clash. (See list on page 131.) This music, although released during the Seventies, has a timeless quality that has allowed it to endure. It still fits in today's world, flowing almost seamlessly in DJ sets between Pearl Jam, REM and Boyz II Men.

To find true, pure Seventies music in the Nineties we must resort to specialty Seventies radio stations like Y107.9 in Chicago. These small microcosms of hell are cropping up all over the country, satisfying hungry listeners of our generation with an "all Seventies, all the time" diet. They serve up Queen, ABBA, Kansas, and Bee Gees music that smacks us like a two-by-four to the head, dislodging firmly repressed memories of days gone by. This music does not fit in today's world. It never fit in, and—Lord willing—it never will. It stands out as a glaring anachronism, like the naive, polyester Brady's from *The Brady Bunch Movie,* cluelessly drifting in a society of rap beats and cellular phones.

Some people have an innate sense and can immediately identify a song as Seventies. (Much like pressing your palm on a stove burner, the body automatically reacts.) Others, who lack this innate sense, need guidance. Never fear, we are here to help.

Identification

There is a quick and sure-fire way to identify a Seventies song: all you need is a boom box and a room full of Nineties, baggy-jeans-wearing, body-pierced teenagers. Today's teens have a keen musical perception that can automatically sense that special Seventies sound.

This skill is partly inborn, as many members of this age group were *in utero* as their mothers attended their first screening of *Saturday Night Fever* and mellowed out to the music of England Dan and John Ford Coley. Today's teens toddled around to the sounds of K.C. and the Sunshine Band and sat proudly in their high chairs as Mom boogied to Casey Casem's top-forty countdown. The effects of this infant exposure to Seventies music on Nineties teenagers cannot be measured and will undoubtedly be a topic for *Stuck in the Seventies Volume II—The Next Generation*. In the meantime, we will use the innate skill of our teenage counterparts to help cure those of the twentysomething generation who are cursed with S.M.I.D.—"Seventies Music Identification Deficit." Pay close attention:

Quite simply, if a teenage subject thinks a song is cool, (*proper, bitchin, def, awesome, righteous, kickin*) it is disqualified for classification as Seventies music. Consider the following examples:

Song	Artist	Teenage Reaction
"Fame" (1975)	David Bowie	Yeah. Okay.
"Take the Money and Run" (1976)	Steve Miller Band	Yes.
"Lay Down Sally" (1978)	Eric Clapton	Sweet.
"Rock and Roll" (1972)	Led Zeppelin	*Ohhhhh Yeeeessssss.*

Evidently, these songs from the Seventies decade do *not* qualify as Seventies music. They instead fall into the "classic rock" category, the music that is woven into the very fabric of our society, uniting the generations from Woodstock to X.

Now consider these songs from the same years:

Song	Artist	Teenage Reaction
"Dream Weaver" (1976)	Gary Wright	*Errrrr.*
"Rhinestone Cowboy" (1975)	Glen Campbell	*Wwwwwhat?*
"Boogie Oogie Oogie" (1978)	A Taste of Honey	Ugggh (froth)
"Baby, Baby Don't Get Hooked On Me" (1972)	Mac Davis	911

It is quickly apparent that these songs from the decade physically hurt today's teens. Thus they solidly qualify as Seventies, the music that divides the generations and threatens to wreck the very fabric of society. These four songs also effectively illustrate four different styles which encompass the full scope of the Seventies genre and our musical depravity:

1. Disco ("Boogie, Oogie, Oogie")

Noted for its incessant beat and the vivid memories it conjures up flashing dance floors and mirror balls. Relatively self-explanatory; see *Saturday Night Fever* soundtrack album or 1977–78 *Billboard Hot 100* for further details.
  • Primary physical reaction: twitching feet and hips.
  • Primary emotional reaction: joy and embarrassment.

2. "Love, American Style" Lounge Songs ("Baby Don't Get Hooked on Me")

Characterized by sickeningly melodic themes and almost elevator music quality. Tony Orlando & Dawn were the royalty of this style ("Tie a Yellow Ribbon Round the Ole Oak Tree," 1973). Other favorites include "Top of the World" (Carpenters, 1973), "Killing Me Softly with His Song" (Roberta Flack, 1973), "Feelings" (Morris Albert, 1975), tragic classics from Barry Manilow, ballads from Bread, and virtually all early Olivia Newton-John songs— "I Honestly Love You" (1974) and "Have You Never Been Mellow" (1975).

- Primary physical reaction: sudden nausea.
- Primary emotional reaction: more nausea.

3. "What Were We Thinking?" Songs ("Rhinestone Cowboy")

Music so horrifying that it deserves its own special niche. These songs are the very definition of bad, yet this is the very reason for their bizarre appeal. They are unmistakably, unforgettably Seventies, the very definition of the decade. Classics include "Disco Duck" (Rick Dees, 1976), "The Streak" (Ray Stevens, 1974), "Run Joey Run" (David Geddes, 1975) "Afternoon Delight" (Starland Vocal Band, 1976), "Mr. Jaws" (Dickie Goodman, 1975), "Kung Fu Fighting" (Carl Douglas, 1974), the preposterous metal and mascara of KISS, every drop of saccharine from Donny and Marie, every syllable uttered by the Village People, and of course, anything from the Partridge Family.

- Primary physical reaction: migraine.
- Primary emotional reaction: fear.

4. Mainstream Seventies Music ("Dream Weaver")

These songs were not bad enough to be completely embarrassing and yet not classic enough to be played on today's rock radio stations. Their beat is not quite disco and their melodies are not quite sickening enough for

"Lounge" classification. They are the fabulously medio-cre, easily overlooked bulk of the Seventies genre. If not for early Nineties radio shows like "The Lost 45s" (hosted by Barry Scott, Sunday nights on WZLX in Boston) and today's "all Seventies, all the time" asylum stations, this core of American music would be completely forgotten. The long list of Seventies mainstream music includes: "Don't Go Breaking My Heart" (Elton John and Kiki Dee, 1976), "Telephone Line" (Electric Light Orchestra, 1977), "Baby Come Back" (Player, 1978), "(Ho, Ho, Ho, It's) Magic" (Pilot, 1975), "The Night Chicago Died" (Paper Lace, 1974), the Kansas classics "Dust in the Wind" and "Carry On My Wayward Son" (1977), everything by ABBA, the ultimate Seventies classic: Queen's "Bohemian Rhapsody" (1976), plus hits by dozens of artists/groups and one-hit-wonders who are destined to remain "Stuck in the Seventies" (see list on page 132).

Professor Cassidy performs "You Light Up My Life"

CHAPTER III: TEST

Identifying Seventies music is truly an art, but after reviewing the classification lessons in Chapter II, anyone can master the basics and perform well on the following Seventies Musicology quiz. Find a teenager, turn on a classic rock station and pull out your deluxe, oak handled, LP disc washing kit: it's time to play "Stuck in the Seventies Name that Tune."

Match these Seventies Grammy Winners with the appropriate category:

1. "Close to You" (The Carpenters, 1970)
2. "Band on the Run" (Paul McCartney & Wings, 1974)
3. "Night Fever" (The Bee Gees, 1978)
4. "Love Will Keep Us Together" (The Captain & Tennille, 1975)
5. "Copacabana" (Barry Manilow, 1978)
6. "Hotel California" (The Eagles, 1977)
7. "What a Fool Believes" (The Doobie Brothers, 1979)
8. "Hot Stuff" (Donna Summer, 1979)
9. "The First Time Ever I Saw Your Face" (Roberta Flack, 1972)
10. "How Deep Is Your Love" (The Bee Gees, 1977)
11. "At 17" (Janis Ian, 1975)
12. "Just the Way You Are" (Billy Joel, 1978)
13. "If You Leave Me Now" (Chicago, 1976)

   a. Seventies Disco Music
   b. Seventies Lounge Music
   c. Seventies "What Were We Thinking?" Music
   d. Seventies Mainstream Music
   e. Classic Rock

Answers:

1. b: Clearly a Lounge Music masterpiece.
2. e: Although not played that frequently today, the McCartney name signifies classic rock.
3. a: One hundred percent pure disco, a cornerstone piece of the Seventies.
4. c or d: Depends upon perspective. Many list "Love Will Keep Us Together" winning Record of the Year as one of the most horrifying events of the decade. Others are more compassionate.
5. c: Most break out into a cold sweat when they hear this one. "Copacabana" won Barry the Best Male Pop Vocal Performance Grammy, leaving Americans bewildered, to say the least. It is best to keep this memory repressed.
6. e: Not just classic rock, but a true anthem of the decade. This is one of five Seventies rock tunes that hold an everlasting "hall of fame" position in music history. Led Zep's "Stairway to Heaven," Lynyrd Skynyrd's "Free Bird," Meatloaf's "Paradise by the Dashboard Light" and Don McLean's "American Pie" join "Hotel California" in this almost biblical status. These five songs are still played at every American party worth going to, their words and guitar riffs known by young and old alike. Perhaps these songs will save the Seventies from total disgrace when future historians look back and try to make sense of it all.
7. e: Gotta love the Doobie Brothers. Check out the inside album sleeve of "Minute by Minute" when you have a chance, then turn to #87 in this book.
8. a: Disco, disco, disco, disco . . . Long live the Queen.
9. b: I actually saw Dirk Venue perform this song in the Pocono Holiday Inn lounge just last year. It hasn't lost its magic—I had to take three trips to the bathroom.

10. d: If it had a beat, it would be disco, but this Bee Gees tune is undanceable. Light the lava lamp and curl up with your honey on the nearest beanbag chair while you listen to this Mainstream masterpiece.

11. d: This is a tough one. Janis' "Learning The Truth At 17" is a bit too meaningful to sing in a lounge, yet is not scary enough to cause people to run from the room screaming; Mainstream by default.

12. e: Sappy, but still a classic. Billy Joel's music has a timeless quality that spans across the decades. He joins our already established list of classic artists and groups whose successful careers include, but are not restricted to, the Seventies.

13. d: This song is on the borderline. While Chicago is a group with "classic" qualities, this particular song sounds more like "Beth" by Kiss than classic rock. In my book, it belongs in the Seventies Mainstream category.

Professor Cassidy demonstrates Voguing

CHAPTER IV: EXPLORATION

The Most Horrifying #1 Songs of the Seventies
Early Decade, 1970–1973

Culturally, the early Seventies looked much like the late Sixties, with Vietnam raging and Kent State fresh in people's minds. This was reflected musically through top albums by Crosby, Stills, Nash & Young, the Beatles, Simon & Garfunkel, Janis Joplin and the Rolling Stones. In fact, many of the nation's most popular songs were true rock classics. At the same time, however, the seed was being planted for the musical debauchery that would plague our country later in the decade. Despite a post-Woodstock atmosphere, the early Seventies saw the rise of "Lounge" music, with Roberta Flack, Neil Diamond, and the Carpenters leading the way. There was also healthy representation from the "What Were We Thinking?" category, with #1 hit songs from Cher and the Partridge Family. Ridiculous melodies and insipid lyrics began to emerge, providing ample raw material for the forces of musical evil that waited patiently in the shadows.

"Alone Again (Naturally)" (Gilbert O'Sullivan)
"Baby Don't Get Hooked on Me" (Mac Davis)
"Ben" (Michael Jackson)
"Black and White" (Three Dog Night)
"Brand New Key" (Melanie)
"Brandy (You're a Fine Girl)" (Looking Glass)
"Candy Man" (Sammy Davis, Jr.)
"Close to You" (Carpenters)
"Cracklin' Rose" (Neil Diamond)
"Delta Dawn" (Helen Reddy)
"Everything Is Beautiful" (Ray Stevens)
"Family Affair" (Sly & the Family Stone)

"Go Away Little Girl" (Donny Osmond)
"Gypsies, Tramps & Thieves" (Cher)
"Half-Breed" (Cher)
"How Can You Mend a Broken Heart" (Bee Gees)
"I Am Woman" (Helen Reddy)
"I Can See Clearly Now" (Johnny Nash)
"I Think I Love You" (Partridge Family)
"Indian Reservation" (Raiders)
"Keep On Truckin' " (Eddie Kendricks)
"Killing Me Softly with His Song" (Roberta Flack)
"Knock Three Times" (Tony Orlando & Dawn)
"Love Train" (The O'Jays)
"Me and Mrs. Jones" (Billy Paul)
"One Bad Apple" (Osmonds)
"Raindrops Keep Fallin' on My Head" (B.J. Thomas)
"Song Sung Blue" (Neil Diamond)
"The First Time Ever I Saw Your Face" (Roberta Flack)
"The Morning After" (Maureen McGovern)
"The Most Beautiful Girl" (Charlie Rich)
"The Night the Lights Went Out in Georgia" (Vicki Lawrence)
"The Way We Were" (Barbra Streisand)
"Theme from Shaft" (Isaac Hayes)
"Tie a Yellow Ribbon Round the Ole Oak Tree" (Tony Orlando & Dawn)
"Touch Me in the Morning" (Diana Ross)
"Top of the World" (Carpenters)

Mid Decade, 1974–1975

By 1974, things had gotten pretty silly. Watergate had shocked the nation and the music scene responded with utter confusion. Like a young teenager whose parents had left town for the weekend, mid-Seventies music was ready to try anything. Olivia Newton-John became chief spokesperson for the "Lounge" movement but was quickly overshadowed by the sheer idiocy of songs like "Kung Fu Fighting," "Convoy," and "The Streak." The stage was set; the time was ripe. Breaking through the insanity to bring order from the chaos was the "savior" of the Seventies. Yes, friends, disco was born.

"Bad Blood" (Neil Sedaka)
"Billy, Don't Be a Hero" (Bo Donaldson & the Heywoods)
"Convoy" (C.W. McCall)
"Feel Like Makin' Love" (Roberta Flack)
"Fly Robin Fly" (Silver Convention)
"Get Down Tonight" (K.C. & the Sunshine Band)
"Have You Never Been Mellow" (Olivia Newton-John)
"He Don't Love You (Like I Love You)" (Tony Orlando & Dawn)
"(Hey Won't You Play) Another Somebody Done Somebody Wrong Song" (B.J. Thomas)
"Hooked on a Feeling" (Blue Swede)
"I Honestly Love You" (Olivia Newton-John)
"Jive Talkin'" (Bee Gees)
"Kung Fu Fighting" (Carl Douglas)
"Laughter in the Rain" (Neil Sedaka)
"Let's Do It Again" (Staple Singers)
"Love Machine" (Miracles)
"Love Rollercoaster" (Ohio Players)
"Love Will Keep Us Together" (The Captain & Tennille)
"Lovin' You" (Minnie Riperton)
"Mandy" (Barry Manilow)
"My Eyes Adored You" (Frankie Valli)

"Rhinestone Cowboy" (Glen Campbell)
"Rock Me Gently" (Andy Kim)
"Rock the Boat" (Hues Corporation)
"Saturday Night" (Bay City Rollers)
"Seasons in the Sun" (Terry Jacks)
"Thank God I'm a Country Boy" (John Denver)
"That's The Way—*Uh-Huh, Uh-Huh*—I Like It"
   (K.C. & the Sunshine Band)
"The Hustle" (Van McCoy)
"The Locomotion" (Grand Funk)
"The Night Chicago Died" (Paper Lace)
"The Streak" (Ray Stevens)
"You're Having My Baby" (Paul Anka)

Late Decade, 1976–1979

Disco careened out of control as the decade came to a close. Nothing was sacred; Beethoven, farm animals, and even *Star Wars* fell victim to the disco-ization craze. Everybody and their brother or sister had a hit song, and the mighty triumvirate of Barry, Maurice and Robin Gibb looked down with glowing approval. These were the years that permanently scarred the Seventies, causing the decade's banishment from the decent, normal course of history. These were the songs that shaped a generation and left America questioning not only itself, but its jumbled past and dim prospects for the future . . .

"A Fifth of Beethoven" (Walter Murphy & the Big
   Apple Band)
"Afternoon Delight" (Starland Vocal Band)
"Baby Come Back" (Player)
"Bad Girls" (Donna Summer)
"Boogie Fever" (Sylvers)
"Boogie Oogie Oogie" (A Taste of Honey)

"Car Wash" (Rose Royce)
"Da Doo Ron Ron" (Shaun Cassidy)
"Dancing Queen" (ABBA)
"December, 1963 (Oh What a Night)" (Four Seasons)
"Disco Duck" (Rick Dees & His Cast of Idiots)
"Disco Lady" (Johnnie Taylor)
"Do Ya Think I'm Sexy" (Rod Stewart)
"Don't Give Up on Us" (David Soul)
"Don't Leave Me This Way" (Thelma Houston)
"Gonna Fly Now"—Theme From *Rocky* (Bill Conti)
"Got to Give It Up" (Marvin Gaye)
"Grease" (Frankie Valli)
"Hot Child in the City" (Nick Gilder)
"Hot Stuff" (Donna Summer)
"How Deep Is Your Love" (Bee Gees)
"I Just Want to Be Your Everything" (Andy Gibb)
"I Will Survive" (Gloria Gaynor)
"I Write the Songs" (Barry Manilow)
"If I Can't Have You" (Yvonne Elliman)
"I'm Your Boogie Man" (K.C. & the Sunshine Band)
"Kiss You All Over" (Exile)
"Knock on Wood" (Amii Stewart)
"Le Freak" (Chic)
"Looks Like We Made It" (Barry Manilow)
"Love Hangover" (Diana Ross)
"MacArthur Park" (Donna Summer)
"(Love Is) Thicker than Water" (Andy Gibb)
"Love You Inside Out" (Bee Gees)
"Night Fever" (Bee Gees)
"Play that Funky Music" (Wild Cherry)
"Please Don't Go" (K.C. & the Sunshine Band)
"Reunited" (Peaches & Herb)

"Ring My Bell" (Anita Ward)
"Shadow Dancing" (Andy Gibb)
"Shake Your Booty" (K.C. & the Sunshine Band)
"Southern Nights" (Glen Campbell)
"Star Wars Theme/Cantina Band" (Meco)
"Stayin' Alive" (Bee Gees)
"Theme from S.W.A.T." (Rhythm Heritage)
"Too Much Heaven" (Bee Gees)
"Torn Between Two Lovers" (Mary MacGregor)
"Tragedy" (Bee Gees)
"Undercover Angel" (Alan O'Day)
"Welcome Back" (John Sebastian)
"When I Need You" (Leo Sayer)
"You Don't Bring Me Flowers" (Barbra Streisand &
    Neil Diamond)
"You Don't Have to Be a Star (To Be in My Show)"
    (Marilyn McCoo & Billy Davis, Jr.)
"You Light Up My Life" (Debby Boone)
"You Make Me Feel Like Dancing" (Leo Sayer)
"You Should Be Dancing" (Bee Gees)
"You're the One that I Want" (John Travolta &
    Olivia Newton-John)

CHAPTER V: AFTERMATH

Has American society recovered from Seventies music? The answer is still unclear, but the general prognosis
is not good.

As we entered the Eighties, there was a brief glimmer
of hope. The disco craze faded rapidly, giving way to
purer, "back to basics" rock and roll. By 1981, Journey,
Reo Speedwagon, Hall & Oates, and John Lennon were
topping the album charts, attempting to cement over the
disco monster that had grasped the industry two years

earlier. But the country's lust for senseless music was strong, and by the end of 1982, groups like Culture Club and Men at Work were climbing the charts, threatening to rekindle the fire that had thoroughly torched the previous decade.

In 1983, Michael Jackson finally offered salvation with his record-breaking "Thriller" LP, legitimizing dance music and creating a new craze for America. The country could be proud once again, reaching back, to the time before the dark years, resurrecting a legitimate hero from the past. In 1984, Bruce Springsteen's "Born in the U.S.A." reflected our pride and Van Halen's "1984" had us "Jump"ing with excitement. In 1985, we fervently shared our enthusiasm as "U.S.A. for Africa" let out the resounding cry "We Are the World!" There they stood, all of our musical heroes, side-by-side, holding hands and proclaiming that a new age had truly begun! Or had it?

Throughout the early Eighties, there stood a force, waiting patiently on the sidelines, a force so influential and so powerful, yet cloaked in a veil of purity and virtue. Starting innocently in 1983 with a great debut album and a string of highly danceable hits, she crept slyly forward. In biblical guise, she emerged "Like A Virgin" in 1985, building momentum and strength in 1986 with "True Blue." Yes my friends, Madonna hit the music scene, and unknowingly paved the way for the forces of musical evil. Foolishness rapidly returned in 1986, as Falco's "Rock Me Amadeus" renewed the attack on classical composers that Walter Murphy had begun a decade earlier. While Madonna was proclaiming "Open Your Heart," the Bangles were "Walking Like an Egyptian" up the charts to #1, once again testing the waters of musical idiocy. George Michael told us to have "Faith," but the enlightened, like Bon Jovi, knew that we were simply "Living on a Prayer." Despite Whitney Houston's aspiration to purify the decade and Michael Jackson's "Bad" attempt at reconciliation, the late Eighties and early Nineties remained firmly in Madonna's control. Before we knew what was happening, we were "Vogueing" on the nation's dance floors, making "The Hustle" look almost sophisticated by comparison.

Vintage rock groups began to make comebacks, trying to chip away at Madonna's solid foothold. Aerosmith, the Rolling Stones, Yes, the Who, but nobody had a chance. The pop charts began to transform, giving birth to Tiffany, Debbie Gibson, and Guns 'N' Roses. Rap exploded onto the scene, and while culturally important, it actually removed melody and instruments from what used to be music. Metallica and Megadeath gave a dangerously sharp new edge to metal, amplifying the decline of the music scene. Madonna stood high above the rest, relishing the tide of commercial decadence she had incited.

And then the unthinkable happened: Donny Osmond reincarnated with his hit song, "Soldier of Love." A remake of Maxine Nightingale's 1976 hit "Right Back Where We Started From" appeared on the charts. From Australia came a Debbie Gibson-type teenager with a Nineties remake of "The Loco-Motion." A strange techno-pop duo hit the scene with a "Stars on 45" sounding hybrid of "Baby, I Love Your Way" and "Free Bird." Deee-Lite's "Groove Is in the Heart" video looked like a "Laugh-In" rerun. People started doing line dances at clubs, wearing brown suits and watching "A Very Brady Christmas." The Seventies nightmare was returning! It was all coming back!

Society sat, teetering on the edge, holding its breath, waiting for something to pull it back from the approaching Seventies abyss. Nirvana tried. REM tried. Pearl Jam tried. Garth Brooks tried. Even Snoop Doggy Dog tried. They pulled and pulled, beckoning us to ignore the irresistible call *Baby, Come Back!* They pleaded, "Please! Please! Try the Seattle sound! Try Country! Try Hip Hop! Try Gangsta Rap! Hell, try Tony Bennett! TRY ANYTHING! Just don't go back to the days of 'Disco Duck,' Beware the 'Boogie Wonderland!'" We almost listened. We were almost ready to run . . . Until that fateful night in 1992 when that AMC Pacer pulled around the corner in Aurora, Illinois.

Wayne and Garth smiled. Wayne and Garth "schwinged." Wayne and Garth cranked the car stereo, thrashed their heads in a musical-moment frenzy and catapulted "Bohemian Rhapsody" back up the pop charts and on to the play list of every Nineties radio station. Almost over night, the free world became *Wayne's World* and all hope for a reprieve from the Seventies vanished.

We fell off the wagon. We began to binge. We didn't stop. We witnessed unbridled breeding of Seventies remakes, K.C. and the Sunshine Band in concert, sideburns, platform shoes, even the Dallas Cowboys winning the Super Bowl twice! People lined up to see the *Brady Bunch Movie* and clamored to watch the Village People scene in *Waynes World 2* on video. We were once again *Dazed and Confused . . .*

They say that history will repeat itself. It has. They say a Seventies revival is inevitable. It is. Musically speaking, it has already happened; the question now is one of size and scope. Will the decadence of Seventies music fade mercifully as the Nineties come to a close? Or will we be doing the Hustle in white leisure suits on New Year's Eve 2000? We don't have the answers, nor can we offer any relief for the twentysomething generation who is still desperately struggling to forget their wanton youth. In either case, I hope this examination of Seventies music will help prepare you for the challenges that rapidly approach. My only advice is to keep an open mind; think carefully about why and how the music of our past affects our present. Let go of the resentment and anger! Cling to the futile hope that someday we'll look back at our high school yearbook pictures and actually believe that we looked cool. Remember: time progresses in mysterious ways. You made it through once, and you can do it again!

Good Luck,
Professor Gibbson Cassidy, Ph.D.

---

13 Things Our Parents Believed Saved Our Generation

13. Flintstone Vitamins.
12. Reverend Billy Graham.
11. Raising the drinking age from 18 to 21 in most states.
10. Nixon's resignation and Carter's defeat.
9. Wheat Germ, granola, and yogurt.
8. Capital punishment.
7. Seat belts with shoulder straps.
6. The station wagon.
5. The documentary *Scared Straight*.
4. Mr. Rogers and "Sesame Street."
3. Republicans.
2. High school guidance counselors with octagonal glasses.
1. The 55 mile-per-hour speed limit.

CLASSIC ARTISTS AND GROUPS
(with hits from the '70s)

AC/DC
Aerosmith
Allman Brothers
Bad Company
Beatles
Blue Oyster Cult
Boston
David Bowie
James Brown
Jackson Brown
Jimmy Buffett
The Cars
Chicago
Eric Clapton
Joe Cocker
Jim Croce
Crosby, Stills & Nash
Doobie Brothers
Bob Dylan
Eagles
Emerson, Lake & Palmer
Fleetwood Mac
Foghat
Aretha Franklin
J. Geils Band
Genesis
The Grateful Dead
The Guess Who
Hall & Oates
Heart
Michael Jackson
Jefferson Starship
Jethro Tull
Billy Joel
Elton John
Journey

The Kinks
Gladys Knight & The Pips
Led Zeppelin
John Lennon
Kenny Loggins
Lynyrd Skynyrd
Paul McCartney
Don McLean
Steve Miller Band
The Moody Blues
Van Morrison
Willie Nelson
Pink Floyd
Smokey Robinson
Kenny Rogers
The Rolling Stones
Rush
Santana
Neil Sedaka
Bob Seger
Paul Simon
Bruce Springstein
Steely Dan
Cat Stevens
Rod Stewart
Styx
Talking Heads
James Taylor
Van Halen
The Who
Dione Warwick
Stevie Wonder
Yes
Neil Young
Frank Zappa
ZZ Top

ARTISTS AND GROUPS WHO ARE "STUCK IN THE SEVENTIES"

ABBA
Ambrosia
Atlanta Rhythm Section
Average White Band
Bay City Rollers
Bee Gees
Stephen Bishop
Bread
Brothers Johnson
B.T. Express
Captain and Tenille
Eric Carmen
Carpenters
David Cassidy
Shaun Cassidy
Chic
Climax
Climax Blues Band
Commodores
Bill Conti
Rita Coolidge
Gene Cotton
Charlie Daniels Band
Mac Davis
Paul Davis
Tony Orlando & Dawn
Kiki Dee
Rick Dees
DeFranco Family
Dr. Hook
Bo Donaldson & The
  Heywoods
Carl Douglas
Earth, Wind & Fire
Walter Egan
Yvonne Elliman
The Emotions
England Dan/John Ford

Coley
Exile
Freddy Fender
Jay Ferguson
Firefall
Roberta Flack
Peter Frampton
Leif Garrett
David Geddes
Gloria Gaynor
Andy Gibb
Andrew Gold
Grand Funk Railroad
Al Green
Henry Gross
Isaac Hayes
Heatwave
Dan Hill
Clint Holmes
Hot
Thelma Houston
The Hues Corporation
Terry Jacks
The Jackson 5
Jigsaw
Kansas
K.C. & The Sunshine Band
Eddie Kendricks
KISS
The Knack
Nicolette Larson
Gordon Lightfoot
Little River Band
Lobo
Looking Glass
Love & Kisses
Mary MacGregor
The Main Ingredient

Melissa Manchester
The Manhattans
Barry Manilow
Marshall Tucker Band
C.W. McCall
Van McCoy
Maureen McGovern
Meatloaf (despite comeback)
Meco
Harold Melvin & Blue Notes
Maria Muldaur
Michael Murphey
Walter Murphy
Anne Murray
Davie Naughton
The New Seekers
Olivia Newton-John
Paul Nicholas
Nilsson
Ted Nugent
Alan O'Day
Ohio Players
The O'Jays
Orleans
Donny & Marie
The Osmonds
Gilbert O'Sullivan
Pablo Cruise
Paper Lace
The Partridge Family
Peaches & Herb
Pilot
Player
Billy Preston
Queen

Gerry Rafferty
Hellen Reddy
Rhythm Heritage
Minnie Riperton
Vickie Sue Robinson
Rose Royce
Rufus & Chaka Khan
Todd Rundgren
Leo Sayer
Boz Scaggs
Sister Sledge
Rex Smith
Phoebe Snow
Sonny & Cher
David Soul
Spinners
The Staple Singers
The Stylistics
Donna Summer
Supertramp
The Sylvers
A Taste of Honey
Tavares
Johnny Taylor
10cc
Three Dog Night
The Trammps
John Travolta
Andrea True Connection
Gino Vanelli
Bob Welch
Barry White
Wild Cherry
Edgar Winter Group

57. Yarn Skills

No living area in the Seventies was complete without at least one fern hanging in a macrame plant hanger. Homemade macrame masterpieces were proudly displayed so that neighbors and friends could be impressed not only with their beauty, but also with the evident skill and patience that went into their creation. I mean, latch-hook rugs were neat, as were those woven God's-eyes that we used to make to adorn our kitchen walls, but these didn't allow the artistic freedom or require the raw talent that macrame did. And macrame was a practical art—we made vests, toilet seat covers, bracelets, belts and even golf club covers (although most dads refused them).

Macrame was big. Among true enthusiasts, bulletins about new knots swept along like hot gossip ("Cathy used this modified *berry knot* in her wall-hanging that must have taken her *hours*.") while everyone's vocabulary expanded to include the requisite macrame terms ("At first I tried a twill hemp but found it was just too coarse to be double-braided.").

My mother went through full-blown macrame fever and took me along with her. I remember a Christmas when we made everyone macrame originals (the best friends and relatives, of course, got the beaded ones). Mom had macrame get-togethers and bought a bunch of "how-to" books, most of which were not very helpful. But they did have pictures of beautiful creations that gave us ideas about what to make. I took it upon myself to make the most difficult piece from the "advanced" section of one of these books, the macrame owl. I even gave up working on my latch-hook rug to do it. I remember starting three or four times, and throwing the mess away

Macrame fever

when it didn't come out right. Finally, after weeks of perseverance, I achieved this ultimate pinnacle of knotting. It was hung prominently on my bedroom wall for everyone—well, my family and five or six of my friends—to see.

In time, sad to say, macrame died out. The cumbersome styrofoam board with the pins in it, which once commanded the top of the kitchen table, was eventually exiled to the garage. The big spools of rope, once cherished and talked about, became those damn things that you tripped over in the hall closet. But my owl stayed, a silent reminder of my macrame conquest, and an artifact to be treasured even as we moved on to new and better fads.

58. The Pet Rock

59. Group Dancing

Group dancing was our first exposure to foreplay. "The Hustle" and "Stayin' Alive" provided a staging area for the more important slow dancing.

In order to take part in the slow dance, the anxious, sweaty-palmed boogier had to be in position when "Three Times a Lady" was cued up by the hip DJ with the unbuttoned silk shirt and the sideburns. To be in position, the anxious, sweaty-palmed boogier had to be on the floor in close proximity to the targeted slow dance partner. "Group Dancing" made getting on the floor easy. Everyone was doing it, so no one could make fun of you.

If you didn't group dance, you couldn't slow dance . . . sounds a lot like foreplay.

60. Scenes from an Elementary School Lunch Room

Clare is on the verge of tears because her school pizza has no cheese on it. School pizza never has enough cheese on it because the cafeteria ladies know that pizza cheese can be balled up and used as projectiles.

Jane is being admonished by one of the "lunch witches" (volunteers assigned to keep order in the cafeteria) for "talking across tables." This practice is widely frowned upon by the lunch witches whose impressive girth leaves no alternative but to frown widely.

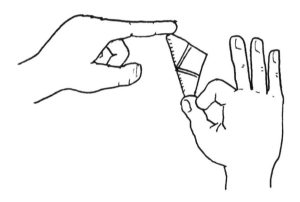

Football showdown

Josh is sobbing. He was playing table football with Scott. With all the savvy of an aerospace engineer, Scott had folded his little triangular football out of sandpaper in order to achieve greater distance and "a better feel" on field goal attempts. With a vigorous flick of his middle finger, Scott shoots the sandpaper football directly through Josh's outstretched thumbs and into his eye. Scott celebrates the victory.

At precisely 12 noon, all the chairs in the cafeteria fall over. The lunch witches jump. The kids pretend not to notice. They are innocent.

Mercifully, it is time for recess. The lunch witches convene and agree that there is no place in the world that they would rather be.

61. Electric Vibrating Football

Most American families have one of these "new-fangled electric games" stashed in their attic or hidden in the back of some musty closet. Electric football introduced a valuable lesson to Seventies children: just because it's electric doesn't mean it's fun.

This game embodied chaos. Both "coaches" would set their little plastic men in formation, one team on offense, the other on defense, then start the vibrating field by turning the vibration volume control knob (usually to "high"). At this point all twenty-two men would begin dancing around the field without direction. The quarterback, twice the size of the other players and outfitted with a special spring-loaded lever arm designed to hurl the cotton ball up to ninety yards at pin-point accuracy, would, when bumped on the helmet by the coach, release the ball. It never went ninety yards and accuracy was not an issue because there was never anyone to throw to. The runners in the backfield were bumping blindly into the stadium stands, the defensive secondary was scattered across the end zone, the line-backers were arm-in-arm doing the do-si-do around the fallen goal posts, and the receivers were usually *behind* the quarterback, doing donuts on their sides.

The frenetic chaos of the game was almost always reflected in the coaches' behavior. Even though rules were virtually impossible to enforce, brothers would get into wrestling matches over off-sides calls, and best friends would claw each other's eyes out over disputes regarding the exact location of the out-of-bounds line. Is it the line on the field or is it the wall where the stands start? The vibrating board would invariably be flipped over and most of the players lost under the couch. The remaining box and instructions were then banished to the attic to serve a life term.

Just because it's electric doesn't mean it's fun.

62. Halter Tops

In the mid-Seventies the preferred vehicle for breast debut was the halter top. Those that had, did, and those that didn't, either didn't have or had good taste.

The pressure to wear halter tops—just to prove you were cool enough to do it—was one of the first significant social tests for girls of our generation. What if the strap unties and Rich sees the truth? What if it spontaneously starts to rain very cold water? What if my parents find out?

Although halter tops posed unsolvable dilemmas to the girls of that era, the boys were vocally unanimous. In a 1975 survey of Mrs. Crossbinder's eighth grade class that asked: "What's the best thing in the world?" halter tops ranked fourth behind recess, substitute teachers, and the Miami Dolphins.

63. The Sports Illustrated Swimsuit Edition

"Hey Ma! Cancel the *National Geographic* subscription!" Jerry yelled while running to lock himself in the bathroom after he retrieved the 1978 *Sports Illustrated* Swimsuit Issue from the mailbox. He couldn't let his mother get her hands on this issue. She'd cancel his subscription for sure if she saw the Cheryl Tiegs' white fishnet swimsuit picture. Forget the Farrah poster! Her gross orange one-piece doesn't even come close to Cheryl's suit, where you can see everything . . . Well, almost everything.

Ah, Cheryl . . .

The face, the body, the swimsuit that ruined an entire generation of young males. No high school cheerleader could compare. Frustration reigned supreme as every male longed for the unobtainable Cheryl. Sadly, phantasmal images of Cheryl, behind closed eyelids, were as close as the boys got. Girlfriends were forever suspicious that their boyfriends were fantasizing about Cheryl when the couples necked in the hidden nooks of the hallway lockers during lunch period . . . *And the girlfriends were right!*

64. Oh Andy, My Andy . . .

Tonight is the night,
He'll finally call,
Said Sally McGee as she stared at the wall.
At that sparkling face
On the back of her door,

Her dream, Andy Gibb,
From ceiling to floor.

Clutching her pillow
In her room all alone,
She had cancelled her plans
Just to sit by the phone.
She had written a letter
Of romance, of bliss,
It was scented with perfurme
And sealed with a kiss.

"Oh Andy, my Andy,"
She said in her bed,
"I know you will call,"
Like the magazine said:
"Just send us a letter
By Saturday noon.
We'll give it to Andy—
He'll get back to you soon."

Sally lay dreaming . . .
His flowing blond hair,
His high sexy voice,
His skin, soft and fair.
"Oh Andy, please love me,"
She said to herself,
As she stared at his records
On their own special shelf.

So many thoughts
For her twelve-year-old brain.
She could feel all the love,
She could feel all the pain.
Sally's eyes had to close,
For she needed her rest.

Still she clung to the phone,
Nestled up to her chest.

"Oh Andy, my Andy,
Our love is so deep . . ."
Said Sally McGee as she fell fast asleep.

65. "Paradise by the Dashboard Light"

When asked how we discovered what it was really like to "slide into home base," our answer was simply: Meatloaf.

Next to *The Joy of Sex*, Meatloaf did most to shape our limited but eager body of carnal knowledge. For the first time, rock and roll was telling us something we had waited years to hear. In "The End," Morrison and the Doors had gone as far as the censors would let them. Robert Plant was always trying to make us believe that something unusual was happening just below the sight lines of the recording engineers in the studio. But it took Meatloaf and his "girlfriend" to give it to us straight: lots of moaning, an inspired Phil Rizzuto play-by-play, and the genuine re-creation of the torrid groin ache that every young teenage boy felt when the central question was asked, "well, what's it going to be boy, yes or no?"

The front seat of Meatloaf's car must have been very large for it served as the setting for both an elephantine love fest and the classroom in which a generation learned a lesson in morality: do what you can to get it but, when necessary, lie.

66. Famous Conversations of the Seventies—Part II

Barbie: Ken, I can't go steady with you anymore. We have to break up.

(Barbie's long, blond freshly-washed-with-Lemon-Up-Shampoo hair is twirled while she sits motionless at her pink table in her open air kitchen.)

Ken: But, Barbie, why?

(Ken is dropped to his knees before Barbie.)

Barbie: Ken, you bore me.

Ken: Bore you? But Barbie, we were made for each other.

Barbie: We may have been cut from the same mold, but you're too perfect. Ken, you're prettier than me.

Ken: But Barbie . . .

Barbie: Ken, look at you. You've got perfect plastic teeth, cheeks, eyes. Ken you even have perfect plastic hair!

Ken: But, doll . . .

Barbie: Ken, face it, you're a plastic dweeb!

Ken: Barbie I can change. Just tell me . . .

Barbie: Kiss off, doll face. I like my men brawny and rugged, with life-like beards and Kung-Fu grips.

Ken: So there is someone else! I knew it. I'll show him for messing around with my girl.

(No one helps Ken up, so he is stuck in a prostrate position sprawled before Barbie.)

Knock! Knock! Knock!

Voice: Yo, Barbs, you in there?

Barbie: Is that you, Joe?

Ken: G.I. Joe? (gulping) Uh-oh . . .

(G.I. Joe is marched in carrying his M-1 rifle. Silver dog tags dangle around his thick neck and rest against his hard-as-rock chest. His bearded and scarred face is turned toward Ken.)

G.I. Joe: Hey, I thought I told you to get lost, plastic breath.

Ken: I . . . I . . .

(Ken remains still, helpless.)

G.I. Joe: Hey Barbs, you want I should shoot the wussy?

Barbie: Just so long as you don't ruin my linoleum tiles with his plastic plasma.

(G.I. Joe's arms are raised, his rifle is pointed at Ken, and—*BAM!*—Ken's head lands in the next room.)

G.I. Joe: Took care of that momma's boy.

Barbie: My hero . . .

A voice intrudes.

Mom: *David!* Stop playing with your sister's doll. It isn't natural!

David: I'm not doing nuthing, Maw!

Mom: Well stop *doing nuthing* and get your butt down here! Now!

David: Aw, all right. God, a kid can't even have any fun anymore.

Who's who?

67. Androgyny

Is there any surprise the twentysomething generation is screwed up with these role models from the Seventies.

Mr. Gender Bender himself, Corporal Max Klinger, who wore his fashionable ensemble, complete with frilly boas, to get Colonel Sherman Potter to sign a Section Eight.

Anatomically inaccurate and appendage-less Ken and G.I. Joe dolls.

Frank N. Furter from *Rocky Horror.*

"A Boy Named Sue."

David Bowie going through "Ch-Ch-Changes."

Dr. Richard Raskind, tennis pro, becoming Dr. Renee Richards, after the expensive operation in Sweden.

The Fruit of the Loom guys.

Flip Wilson as Geraldine or Geraldine as Flip Wilson.

And what sex is the Pillsbury Dough-Boy anyway? A male? *Prove it!*

---

13 Best Seventies Bumperstickers

13. Mafia Staff Car: U Toucha My Car, I Breaka U Face
12. Have Wife 40. Will Swap for 2:20s
11. Call Me Ms.
10. I Don't Touch Your Woman—You Don't Touch My Car!
9. South of the Border.
8. Honk If You're horny!
7. Beep, Beep, Yer Ass.
6. Have a Nice Day! (The big yellow smiling face.)
5. Keep on Truckin'.
4. Warning: I break for Animals.
3. Impeach Nixon!
2. I found it!
1. Don't Blame Me: I Voted For McGovern

68. Swingers

Ahh swingers—those sexually adventurous and liberated couples free from the constraints of matrimonial pledges. Let's see how swinging in the Seventies influenced the typical American family, the Greens . . .

Ten-year-old Lester Green and his best friend Chuck.

"Hey Chuckles, did ya hear about the Goodmans?" Lester asked.

"You mean the people who live down the street in the yellow house?" Chuck replied.

"Yup."

"What about them?"

"I heard my Mom and Pop talking about them. They're swingers."

"Let's go!"

"Where?" Lester asked.

"To the Goodmans'!"

"Why?"

"Dahhh . . . Because they got swings."

"Don't be such a dink. They're swingers. They . . . ah . . . trade themselves."

"Trade themselves?" Chuck asked.

"Yeah. Like, you know. Mr. Goodman trades Mrs. Goodman for someone like Mrs. Ortmeyer, and then they *do it* and stuff."

"Awesome! I'll trade you my mom for your 1967 Yastrzemski baseball card. What do ya say?"

"God, you're such a dork sometimes."

Mr. and Mrs. Green.

"Honey, I was thinking," Mr. Green said thoughtfully. "It's about time we got to know our neighbors better. We ought to have the Goodmans over tonight for, say, dinner?"

"Good idea darling. I'll fire up the hot tub."

Thirteen-year-old Lori Green on the phone with her best friend Darlene.

"Darlene, trust me. Swinging is simple. You like *my* Glenn better than I do, right? And I like *your* Johnny better than you do. So you break up with Johnny and I break up with Glenn. Then, I'll tell Brian to tell Glenn that you like him and you wanna go out with him, and you tell Lee to tell Johnny that I like him and that I wanna go out with him. See, swinging's so easy. They'll never know, I swear."

69. Seventies Sex Education

Inspired by Shere Hite's book, *The Hite Report: The Nationwide Study of Female Sexuality* (Macmillan, 1976), we have launched our own clinical study to lend our book the aura of respectability it deserves and to provide a lasting value to you, our esteemed reader. Our paramount concern and research quandary was framed into one question: where did you first learn about and see the sexual "privates" of the opposite gender?

As we started our anonymous phone survey, we received several ambiguous answers like, "drop dead," "I gave at the office," and the ever popular, "What? Who is this? I know, is this . . ." However, after 3,557 phone calls and a few dozen respondents, we, the intrepid researchers, have reached a definitive conclusion, we think. First, the results:

Source	Percentage Responding to the Source	
	Male	Female
Respondent Saw "Privates" The Normal Way From:		
• Pictures or drawings in school sex education books	0%	0%
• Seeing parents, siblings, relatives, friends naked in the shower, getting dressed, behind the garage, etc.	5%	91%
Respondent Saw "Privates" The Seventies Way From:		
• The anatomically correct Little Joey Stivic doll	1%[1]	4%
• The anatomically castrated G.I. Joe doll	0%	1%

---

[1] The researchers didn't bother to ask and quickly hung up. They didn't want to know.

- The anatomically incorrect Barbie doll   14%   0%
- The anatomically and genetically messed up
  Ken doll   0%   1%
- Older sister's issue of *Cosmopolitan* with the
  Burt Reynolds, you-can-almost-see-
  everything, spread   0%   2%
- Older brother's *Playboy* magazine stashed
  under his electric football game   12%   0%
- The *Sports Illustrated* Swimsuit Issue that
  made fishnet bathing suits and Cheryl Tiegs
  famous   24%   0%
- An R-rated movie watched from a tree
  outside the drive-in fence   15%   0%
- Jacqueline Bisset's wet t-shirt scene in
  The Deep   14%   0%
- The string bikini   13%   0%
- Subliminal messages: phallic images hidden
  in the ice cubes and liquor in magazine ads   1%   1%
- What's a private?   1%   0%

Totals	100%	100%

Conclusion: it is the Eleventh Wonder of the World that the males of the twentysomething generation can even spell the word "sex."

70. Shaft

My fourteen-year-old brother, Steve, still fumes to this day when he remembers the Saturday he let me (a ten-year-old) tag along with him and three of his friends as we left our suburban town and took the train into Boston. (He had no choice, because I threatened to tell Mom that he destroyed my best Matchbox cars with a hammer.) Trips into Boston were top secret, clandestine operations plotted with the skill necessary to insure that our parents never found out. Punishments consisting of

Shaft

one month groundings—with no TV—were common for
such an offense.

So what were five white kids from the suburbs planning to do in Boston? To go to a theater that let under-
aged adolescents into R-rated blaxploitation movies, of

course! We were tired of seeing a white, bald-headed cop speak street ("Who loves ya, baby?"). We wanted the real thing. And private eye John Shaft was it, man.

After the movie, while walking up the driveway to our house, with Isaac Hayes' theme song ricocheting through my skull, I sauntered my best Shaft walk, and approached my mother who was tending her garden. I ignored the pebbles that my brother threw at my head.

"Did you boys have fun at the library?" Mom inquired.

"Hey, Mom—who's the kid that's the sex machine to all the chicks?"

My brother stopped throwing the pebbles and cringed, immediately recognizing this excerpt from the "Shaft" theme song: he knew what was coming.

"What did you just say?" Mom asked me.

"He said nothing, Ma. Come on ya little dink," Steve said, grabbing the back of my shirt, trying to pull me away.

"Stay loose, Bro. Why you all hyped up?"

"Steve, why is he talking like this? Where have you two been?"

"No . . . Nowhere," Steve stammered. "Honest."

"Don't jive her, baby. This cat took me on a heavy trip DOWNTOWN."

"Downtown? Steve explain this now."

"Cool down, bad Mama. We cruised into Boston to see my man, Shaft."

"Boston!" Mom chased Steve around the yard and into the house.

"Right on! Lay it on him, funky Mama! Wait till THE MAN gets home, then he's really gonna get it—Sucka!"

From that point on, Christie Love, George Jefferson, Thelma and J.J. Evans, Raj, Rerun, Dwayne, Morris Thorpe, "Boom Boom" Washington, Mama, and even Fred Sanford, became a staple in my TV diet. The

Beastie Boys, New Kids on the Block, Vanilla Ice, and Young Black Teenagers must have been fed the same stuff too.

71. Billy Beer

Humans are intrigued by royalty. England's Princess Diana, Monaco's Prince Rainier and Princess Caroline, and Jordan's Queen Noor have become real-life story-book characters. Americans—lacking the tradition of some of these countries—have been forced to "manufacture" their own royalty. This American royalty is often families that have lived in the White House: John and Samuel Adams, Teddy and Franklin Roosevelt, John Kennedy . . . Billy Carter.

The Adams, Roosevelts and Kennedys put their names on libraries, hospitals, and charitable foundations. Billy put his on a beer can. Billy Beer: The beverage by and for Seventies royalty.

72. Beer Can Collecting

In the early morning of October 12, 1977, Little Phil Deutch woke in a sweaty panic. He had been touched by a vision. Little Phil had been visited by a woman—a lithe, beautiful, perfect woman. Her name was Vicky, the Maid of the Loch, and she lived on a beer can, the only

can Phil was missing in his near-complete Tennent's
Girls collection.

After his dream it was clear that Little Phil would do
anything for Vicky, the Maid of the Loch. He would
sacrifice his entire Olde Frothingslosh collection, or even
his unopened domestic 8 oz. collection. He would offer
anything except his only cone top; the can he found
under the back seat of his Grandfather's Edsel. Phil was
frantic.

Phil met Chris Pasko—the beer can magnate and heir
to his older brother's formidable collection—after
school. Chris was widely considered to be the shrewdest
and most ruthless negotiator on the playground. Little
Phil was no match for Pasko, but Pasko owned Vicky,
the Maid of the Loch.

Little Phil opened with a gentleman's offer: an unopened 12 oz. Foster's stretch can and a slightly damaged '58 Rheingold.

Pasko laughed in his face.

Little Phil threw in the Olde Frothingslosh collection. His offer was met with scorn.

Desperate, Little Phil offered the cans that made up the heart and soul of his collection.

Pasko smelled blood. Phil began to shake. "My sources inform me," Pasko said with the premature tone of an infuriatingly superior Wall Street banker, "that your pitiful collection has one can worthy of my attention."

Little Phil choked back an urgent sob. Pasko attacked his helpless prey: "Your pristine 1947 Miller High Life cone top for Vicky. I will accept nothing less."

Little Phil's little head was spinning, his little eyes stung from the salt in his tears, "Okay, Okay, the cone top for Vicky, I have no choice, I had a dream."

The love of a woman—even an aluminum one—always has a steep price.

73. Zoom

Lustful, frothing, pre-teen envy . . .

"That's ZOOM, Box-Three-Five-Oh, Boston-Mass, Oh-Two-One-Three-Four . . ."

Late afternoon, PBS, scorching childhood jealousy . . .

"Let's roll out the barrel, we're gonna find out what's inside today . . ."

What does Bernadette have that I don't? I can read mail, sing, and smile! I belong up there on the screen with those kids! Why can't I be on TV like them?

"Do a ZOOM do, do a ZOOM do, do a ZOOM do . . ."

Ahhh . . . Imagine going to the TV station every day after school . . . Picture the faces of your friends when they see you on the air . . . Envision life as a bonafide celebrity . . . But *Noooo* . . . not me . . . I don't live in Boston. I can't get an audition!

"C'mon and ZOOM a ZOOM a ZOOM a ZOOM . . ."

Thirsting vengeful spite . . .

We watched it every day. Smiling through the skits, laughing through the letters, and silently hoping for somebody to drop dead, creating a sacred vacancy that only our talents could fill.

Are we a competitive, cynical generation?

Ask Bernadette and her damned twisty arms.

74. Judy Blume

Judy Blume hit all the hot topics: breast growth, menstruation, nocturnal emissions, and cooties. Her seminal work, *Are You There God? It's Me, Margaret* was the bible for young girls budding into womanhood. Seventh grade girls were often caught performing the "we must, we must, we must increase our bust" exercises behind the swingset, and "Teenage Softies," the fictitious brand name for feminine pads made especially for rookies, became the big joke for most seventh grade boys.

Blubber and *Tales of a Fourth Grade Nothing* were fine for the tame stories about adolescence, but *Forever* was the book that offered the hungry young reader the really good stuff. Open to page 185 and re-read about "Ralph." It's still pretty good.

75. Psalm 1975

The Lord looked down upon the land and saw a time of desolation. He sensed the blaze of ludicrous fabric patterns, felt the rumble of Chrysler tires and heard the incessant pounding of disco drums. He probed the sacred airwaves, astonished by the success of "Laverne & Shirley," noting particularly the elevation of Lenny and Squiggy to heroic status. "Thou shalt not worship false idols." The Lord remembered his words clearly and was now puzzled that they had been so quickly forgotten. He gazed lovingly upon his children, in their blissful ignorance, and concluded quickly that things were not so good.

So, the Lord set forth upon the earth a savior, a man who could rise above the chaos and bring order from disarray; a man whose sense of humor and comedic judgment would break through the wretched confusion of late-Seventies prime time; a man who could reshape television and use its mighty power to reverse the torrent of bad taste and cheesiness that plagued society. With a mighty hand, the Lord brought forth Lorne Michaels unto NBC.

Lorne gathered his flock, the disciples who would bring his vision forth and spread the word of intelligent and inspired humor to the simple masses: Dan Aykroyd, John Belushi, Chevy Chase, Jane Curtin, Garrett Morris, Loraine Newman, Gilda Radner, and Bill Murray. And he said to his flock, "Go forth! Not on Sunday morning, but on Saturday Night; not dead, but live, not thirty minutes, but ninety; not restrained, but free and unrestricted."

And with these words, the world saw an awesome change. Roseanne Roseannadanna rose to conquer Charlie's Angels; the Samurai warrior vanquished the

Six Million Dollar Man. The Land Shark devoured Sonny and Cher. Humankind witnessed an epic revolution; a new age of comedic reason had begun.

Despite the persistence of "America's Funniest Home Videos" and the very existence of Urkel, the Lord still has reason for hope as the twentieth century comes to a close. "Saturday Night Live" still perseveres. Yea though it struggles, the potential for sensibility still glimmers. We hope and pray that the covenant between Lorne Michaels and NBC will not be broken. Draft with strength and freshness and without hemorrhoid jokes, oh mighty writers. Watch with patience, oh steadfast viewers.

Rest in peace, John and Gilda.

Amen.

76. All in the Family . . . Tree

Archie Bunker was the first television character to openly acknowledge his need to use the bathroom. Indeed, the nation heard its first toilet flush at 704 Howser Street. But, "All in the Family" did not use bathroom humor like many of its contemporary sitcoms, instead it boldly dealt with real adult topics, changing the very direction of television comedy. Norman Lear was the proud papa of the show, and lucky for us, his fertility did not stop with the Bunkers. Lear offspring began popping up all over the tube: "The Jeffersons" were neighbors who "moved on up to the East Side." Archie's cousin "Maude" had an extremely successful spin-off, and Maude's housekeeper Florida had her own "Good Times" soon afterwards. Although "Mary Hartman, Mary Hartman" was not a blood relative of "All in the

Family," she was a stepsister at heart who strongly upheld the family heritage. We salute you, Norman Lear,
with an anatomically correct Emmy Award.

Mary Hartman in repose

77. *

---

* The year 1977 is a blight on our generation. The release of *Saturday
Night Fever* sealed our destiny, assuring our banishment from the decent
natural course of history. Members of Lynyrd Skynyrd perished in a plane
crash, the Bee Gees won a Grammy, and "Barry Manilow Live" appeared
on the album charts. Some even blame us for the death of Elvis Presley on
Tuesday, August 16. For these reasons, among many others, we refuse to
recognize the number 77.

78. Land of the Lost

Marshall, Will and Holly,
On a routine expedition,
Met the greeeeatest earthquake
Ever known!

With these opening lines, we watched a family's rubber raft plunge over a waterfall and into a crevice in the earth's crust. Through the miracle of appallingly bad special effects, we traveled back through time with them to the strange, prehistoric "Land of the Lost."

Yes, we watched a Saturday morning television program that featured a baby Brontosaurus called Dopey, witless evil lizards called Sleestacks and a little guy in a fur suit named Chaka. Each week, there was another adventure set in a prehistoric valley, with live volcanos and hungry flying reptiles. We looked on anxiously as the hapless family contended with a variety of savage threats, more often than not constructed in polystyrene at seemingly small expense to the show's producers. Yet somehow "The Land of the Lost" had its charm: Could we have identified subtly with the Marshall family, adrift in a strange brown world filled with man-made monstrosities? This question may be better left to our generation's psychoanalysts.

Much in the Seventies reflected our affinity for prehistoric times. There were snap-together models called Prehistoric Figures (my favorites were the Saber-Tooth Tiger and Triceratops). We anxiously awaited *Godzilla* movie festivals on Saturday afternoons. "The Flintstones" (produced largely in the Sixties) were an essential part of every kid's afternoon television schedule and morning vitamin regime. Sid and Marty Krofft gave us "Sigmund and the Sea Monsters" and the superbly inane "H.R. Pufnstuf." (As I recall, the froglike H.R. Pufnstuf costume required that the actor inside literally jump up and down in order to make the mouth move, a fact that always captured my attention more consistently than did the goings-on in the show.)

So what became of these innocent, poorly executed "monsters" of our youth? Well, there was an ill-fated remake of "Land of the Lost" recently, but what chance does a Sleestack have against the vicious, chillingly realistic Velociraptors of *Jurassic Park?* Holly Marshall always made it back to the cave when pursued by Grumpy, the irritable Tyrranosaurus Rex, but she wouldn't last a second with one of Steven Spielberg's razor-fanged, digitally enhanced creatures. But, hey, dinosaurs are more popular than *ever*, so what about it, Steven? A $45 million *H.R. Pufnstuf* movie? Stranger things have happened. . . .

79. Currency that Failed

The federal government has enough trouble cutting a good image without the added flak over new-fangled money that didn't make it in the marketplace.

The Treasury eased into the "new money" thing when they prudently changed the ingredients of the nickel, dime, and quarter because the value of the coin's metal was worth more than the face value of the coin. Wise move.

Next, they introduced the bicentennial coin set. The hokey quarters, half-dollars, and dollars rode the wake of patriotic celebration brought in by the tall ships on our country's 200th birthday. Although some prepubescent arbitrageurs took a profit on school-yard exchange rates inflated by the whole bicentennial hubbub, it was soon discovered that these coins, like all the old ones, still only bought one pack of baseball cards.

With the modest success of these coins in its back-pocket, the Treasury loosened its tie, mumbled "In God We Trust" and got really crazy.

The Susan B. Anthony dollar. Treasury folks must all be of hearty stock because no one, it seems, gave any thought to the oppressive weight of this coin. Muggers liked these dollars because anyone carrying more than two would walk with a pronounced listing to one side and never be able to outrun a criminal before jettisoning the valuable load. Aerial balloonists used these coins as

ballast—effectively gaining altitude while increasing at-
tendance at some of the lesser-known balloon meets,
and it is said that a group of decathletes petitioned the
Olympic Committee to replace the discus with a slightly
modified version of the Susan B. Anthony dollar for the
1980 games in Moscow.

The two dollar bill. Perhaps anticipating the inflation
of the Carter-years, the treasury released the $2 bill in
1976. It seems clear that these money mavericks disre-
garded the old phrase "queer as a two dollar bill." It
seems clearer that the American public did not forget
that phrase as most money carriers chose to suffer under
the load of two Susan B. Anthony's than present a wallet
full of "funny money" or "queer cash."

80. Mood Rings

"Dana-Beth, my boyfriend just gave me the coolest
thing. Look!"

"What, the ring? It's ugly."

"No, it's *really* cool. It's called a 'mood ring.' It changes
color to tell you what kind of mood you're in. When you
feel happy, it's purple, and when you're really tense, it
turns black, and when it turns green, it means—"

"Well, what does it mean now? It's kind of brownish."

"Uh, I don't know."

"It's really ugly."

"Oh, Dana-Beth, you just don't get it. You're such a
retard."

Like so many gimmicks of the Seventies, the mood
ring was an attempt to blend science with fashion.
Ostensibly, this piece of jewelry sensed a person's

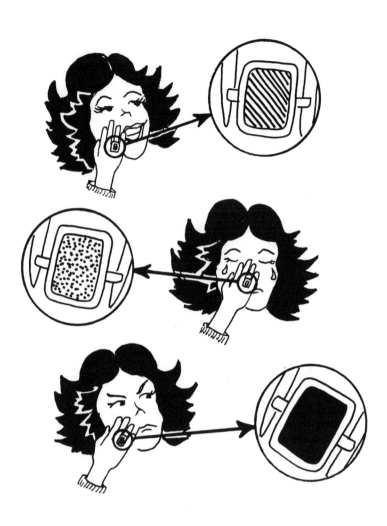

The many faces of the mood ring

emotional state and turned an appropriate color in response. Of course, everyone more or less knew that it was just changing color with body temperature, but it enjoyed a brief reign of novelty on the school bus and playground. The serious mood ring set (typically owned by the girls who carried notebooks with pictures of unicorns and rainbows on them) tried to keep the fad alive by diversifying into mood bracelets and necklaces. Fortunately for the rest of us, their efforts failed, and mood jewelry died a quick, timely death. Or so we thought.

81. Amy Carter

To be the president's daughter...How wicked awesome! My life was so dull and boring in 1977. I was in the fifth grade, and I did the same thing day in and day out. After homework on week nights I gossiped on the phone until bedtime at ten o'clock. On weekends, I hung out at the mall and shopped for 24K simulated gold charms or pictures of John Travolta to add to my collection. I bet Amy's life was way cooler than my life.

Oh sure, Amy had to shake hands with a bunch of dignitaries at those stuffy dinners every now and then, and put up with nerdy parents who liked to show off their teeth a lot, but imagine all the neat things that come along with her first-daughter status. Those cool Secret Service agents watch her every move and protect her. Like, if that boy Ken pulled my hair again on the playground, I bet they'd shoot him on the spot.

Amy could also get her mother to invite Robbie Benson, or better yet, the Bay City Rollers to a White House dinner. They would sing "I Only Want to Be with You" right to me! How dreamy! What a neat life! I could sleep in a canopy bed or throw a slumber party in Mrs. Lincoln's bedroom or fly to malls around the world in Air Force One or call my friends on the red phone or even have one of Daddy's aides do my homework . . . I could do whatever I wanted, because I would be the President's daughter.

But, maybe it's not so great. I mean, I couldn't spend all day at the mall with my friends. In a couple of years, I'd have to go back to that peanut farm. And I'd be sort of ugly and geeky, especially with those thick glasses and freckles. I don't think any amount of fluffing, teasing, and moussing could add a wing to Amy's stringy strawberry-blonde hair. If I got a pimple, the whole world would know about it. Plus, I'd have to wear her plain clothes, because I don't think my Danskin top and wrap-around skirt or my two dollar K-Mart terricloth shorts and tube top would be a hit in Washington. And worst of all, there's that weird Uncle Billy.

God, I'd be such a nerd. No one would like me. And everyone would make fun of me. Maybe I don't want to be Amy Carter after all.

Amy Carter: cool or cursed?

82. Hunks and Hunkettes

We thought about them every waking moment. They were always in our dreams. We belonged to their fan clubs. We created collages from every picture we could lay our hands on. We worshipped these celebrities. In tribute to the many ways they screwed up our lives, we created this word search game, just like the ones we spent many hours doing when we were kids. (Don't forget: the names below can appear backwards, upside down and/or diagonally. The answers are on page 172.)

Catherine Bach
Scott Baio
Robbie Benson
Blondie
Bluto
Sonny Bono
Shaun Cassidy
Cher
Peter Criss
Pam Dawber
Bo Derek
Joyce DeWitt
Susan Dey
Tamara Dobsen
Erik Estrada
Farrah Fawcett
Fonzie
Peter Frampton
Andy Gibb
Pam Grier
Kate Jackson
Michael Jackson
Bruce Jenner
Elton John
Tom Jones
Kojak

Lee Majors
Joe Namath
Paul Newman
Ryan O'Neal
Marie Osmond
Freddie Prinze
Burt Reynolds
Brooke Shields
O.J. Simpson
Jaclyn Smith
Suzanne Somers
David Soul
Mark Spitz
Stallone
Paul Stanley
Parker Stevenson
Rod Stewart
Donna Summer
Denny Terrio
Cheryl Tiegs
John Travolta
Jon Voight
JJ Walker
Raquel Welch
Billy Dee Williams

Word Find

```
P E T E R C R I S S M A I L L I W E E D Y L L I B U R
T F R E D D I E P R I N Z E L T O N J O H N H O R N Y
A S A L I V E D E O P D T J A C L Y N S M I T H X E S
N D Q R B E H T T J H Y I V T A M A R A D O B S E N M
S C U J R P M A E A A G P A U L S T A N L E Y D K E I
H H E R U A S I R M L I S Q H C A B E N I R E H T A C
M E L O C U H D F E L B K A T E J A C K S O N B T O H
A R W D E L A F R E I B R O O K E S H I E L D S J C A
S Y E S J N U C A L C E A P E S A D A R T S E K I R E
C L L T E E N K M W U S M B U Y U G D A V I D S O U L
O T C E N W C A P A C S O T H I S S E X I S G O O D J
T I H W N M A J T L E E N B O O K T A G R E G D A N A
T E B A E A S O O L B J T A G A I N S N R E D R U M C
B G O R R N S K N Y B U R T R E Y N O L D S H I R E K
A S D T O H I M O M C K E B L U T O J K O E M B A S S
I H E U T B D F U C H E I Z N O F W S O N N Y B O N O
O I R R E T Y N N E D A D B O N U S I T N X X X J N N
R M E R R C F T O M J O N E S E I K M I A V Q J A Y K
Y A K I E L I S A M D F O F W C B N P J S L O N Y C S
A T E A K L U V T O S U L Z V I N A S A U E L I S I C
N T I H L C B K T D B O B R E T T H O F M R X O G S O
O Y P P A M G R I E R L E T H I S T N U M D H S N H T
N S E X W A I R T I M E V I B O O K I S E H A O E E T
E E E E J O E N A M A T H R R F U N N Y R P O W R X M
A X E S J O H N T R A V O L T A T E L L Y O U R B N A
L S Q U A W K S U Z A N N E S O M E R S B U D D Y E Y
P A R K E R S T E V E N S O N N O S N E B E I B B O R
```

Answers to the Hunk and Hunkette word search:

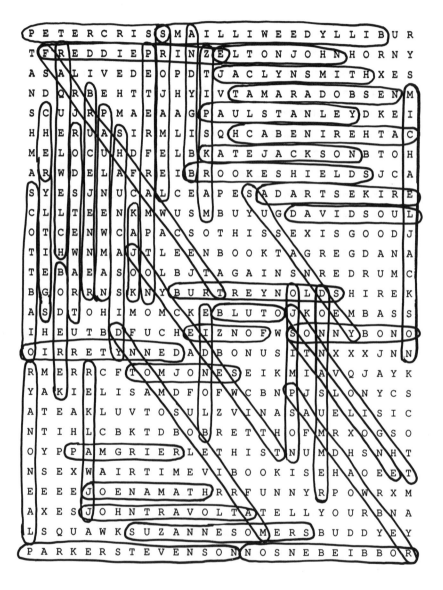

Does this picture arouse you?

83. Subliminal Seduction

No, you didn't become stimulated and aroused because you were thinking about Burt Reynolds' hairy chest, or Catherine Bach's (a.k.a. Daisy Duke's) short-shorts, or Billy Dee Williams' suave, debonair voice, or Suzanne Somers' bouncy and buoyant attributes. The reasons are more sinister.

Do you feel the urge to worship the devil or to hire MBAs or to buy this book again or to tell a buddy about it? Is sex good? R U horny?

If you answered "yes" to any of these questions, seek immediate help. Once again, you have been unknowingly seduced by subliminal messages as you completed the Hunk and Hunkette Word Search. Growing up with phallic figurines, copulating couples, and sex messages hidden in soda, liquor, cigarette, and even children's toy advertisements has damaged your ability to guard against these dangerous influences that attack your subconscious. Remember? Wilson Bryan Key had warned us about this practice in his book *Subliminal Seduction*.

Until you see your analyst, you should avoid all potential subliminal stimuli, because this legacy of our generation makes us easy prey. Do not play your records backwards, do not look at magazine ads for more than two seconds, and with remote in hand, do not watch commercials for more than five seconds. You can watch Madonna or Bell Biv DeVoe videos, however, because there is nothing subliminal about them.

84. Mom! Susie Threw Up!

It was beyond my wildest dreams. Nothing could have been sweeter than the sight of my fourteen-year-old sister's green face! Hunched over, clutching her gut, eyes rolling backward in her head! It was beautiful revenge.

My twelve-year-old mind was delirious with joy. I was loving the movie, every minute of it! It was called *Earthquake*. It was filmed with this really neat effect called "Sensurround" so the whole theater shook. I gripped my seat and held on for the ride. It was so cool! Dad was having a great time too, until . . .

Susie got sick! Susie got sick!

All over the seat in front of her. This Sensurround thing was better than I thought. I couldn't decide—who should I tell first? Her boyfriend? (I felt like throwing up every time they kissed—it was only fair.) Maybe my little brother Danny—nah, he's too young to fully appreciate it. Mom? Yeah, I'll tell Mom first. She always says I should be more like Susie, more mature and responsible. This will show her who's really more mature!

Oh yeah—here comes another quake! Hang on!!! I can't wait to come back and see *Earthquake* again. I can't wait till the next Sensurround movie! I hope every movie from now on has it! And I hope Susie goes to every one and keeps on getting sick! Yes sir, that would be the best of all!

---

13 Seventies TV Shows Best Forgotten

13. "C.P.O. Sharkey" with Don Rickles
12. "Lucas Tanner" with David Hartman
11. "The Bob Crane Show" with Colonel Hogan
10. "Logan's Run" with Gregory Harrison
 9. "Don Adams' Screen Test" with Maxwell Smart
 8. "The Ropers" *sans* Janet, Chrissy, and Jack
 7. "Mulligan's Stew" with Elinor Donahue
 6. "Bob & Carol & Ted & Alice" with the swingers
 5. "James At 15" with Lance Kerwin
 4. "The Don Knotts Show" with Deputy Barny Fife
 3. "Baa Baa Black Sheep" with Robert Conrad
 2. "The Gong Show" with Chuck Barris
 1. "The Bobbie Gentry Show"

85. Vinyl Love

"Daddy, what's vinyl?"

"I'm sorry sweetheart, what did you say?"

"What's vinyl, you know, like when you were a kid. What's an 'Elpee?'"

"Come on over here."

Dana climbed onto her father's lap, her inquisitive five-year-old eyes opened wide with wonder. She took the audiophonic receiver nodes out of her ears and put her new "Walk-microprocessor" down on the table, ejecting the two-inch sound disc from its drive.

Holding the disc up to her father she proclaimed, "I love my new music collection!" Her small piece of plastic and silicon held the equivalent of fifty record albums.

"When I was a kid," her father explained, "I needed two big crates to carry around my music collection."

"Really?" Dana was amazed. "So an Elpee is some kind of box?"

"No honey, no. Here, let me show you." Dad reached behind him and pulled an antique album from the shelf. It was Styx "Grand Illusion," vintage 1977.

"This is an LP. This holds the music, like your disc."

"No it does not!" Dana giggled, "Cut it out, Daddy!"

"No, really honey, look at these grooves, see these hold the songs, well, sort of." His little girl was finding this quite amusing. A gleeful smile swept across her face. "Wait, Dana, take a look at this." He pulled a dusty 8-track tape from his desk drawer. "See, this also held music back in the Seventies. It's kind of like your disc, only bigger." Dana took the cartridge in her hand with interest. Dad continued, "The only problem with 8-tracks was that you couldn't rewind the . . ."

"Re-WHAT?" Dana chimed in.

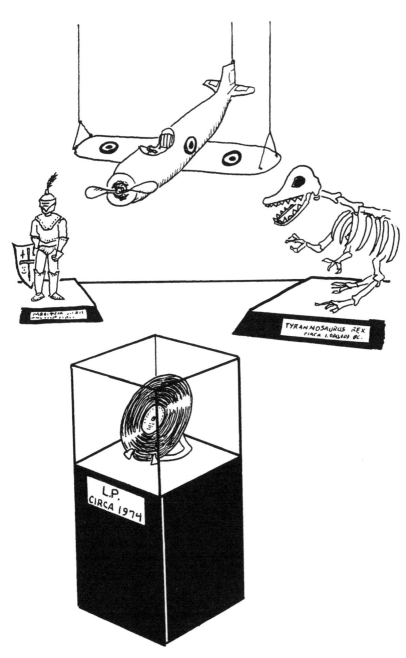

Requiem for an LP

Dad paused. It was no use. "Never mind, sweetheart, it's not important." He lifted Dana off his lap and sent her off to ask Mom about Elpees and 8-tracks.

Dad was tired and a bit depressed. He missed the "good old days" when music was music and records were big. He closed his eyes and pictured the Yes album cover masterpieces by Roger Dean that once filled his room. He longed for the comforting skips and hisses of his worn copy of Fleetwood Mac's "Rumours." Dana would never know the wonder of vinyl love, and Dad asked himself, is she truly better off? He leaned back in his chair and sighed while the imperfect crackling sounds of his imperfect generation swam about his head.

86. Dumb Jokes

Seventies jokes were bland and witless. We never really had a sense of humor during that decade. It took us years to develop and hone the sense of humor we share today. Compare the following jokes from the Seventies to the current Bill Clinton and O.J. Simpson jokes. Aren't you glad these dumb jokes are long forgotten?

1. Knock, knock.
   Who's there?
   Banana.
   Banana who?

   Knock, knock.
   Who's there?
   Banana.
   Banana who?

Knock, knock.
Who's there?
Orange.
Orange who?
Orange-ya glad I didn't say banana!

2. When is it all right for a woman to slap a midget?
   —When he says, "Gee, your hair smells terrific!"

3. What is long and hard and full of semen?
   —A submarine.

4. How do you catch a streaker in a church?
   —Grab him by the organ.

5. What do you call it when a cow gets an abortion?
   —Decaffeinated.

6. What do you call a cow masturbating?
   —Beef Strokinoff.

7. What do you get when a cow jumps over the barbed wire fence?
   —Utter destruction.

8. What do you call Kool-Aid and potassium cyanide?
   —A Jonestown Cocktail

9. Have you heard that Nixon saw *Deep Throat* six times, but he still can't get it down Pat?

87. Just Say . . . Something

Pot, reefer, reef, weed, J, doobie, doobage, dube, bone, smoke, hooter, roach, Mary Jane, Acapulco Gold, home grown, hemp, shit, dope, nickel, dime, oz . . . There! I said it!

For those who didn't know, didn't care, didn't care to know, or don't remember, I'm here to tell you: people smoked marijuana during the Seventies.

That's right! Parents, teachers, sisters, brothers, adults, teens, jerks, jocks, teams, frats, brats, geeks, freaks, blondes, brunettes, redheads, nerds, brains, and even Judge Ginsburg—everybody tried it, bought it, and tried to hide it. They were stoned, high, buzzed, wasted, toasted, partying, playing, tripping, flying, frying, blazing, crazing, toking, shot-gunning, and smoking with bongs, bowls, party bowls, blips, and pipes! In the woods, on the beach, in the house, at the park, in the yard, by the school, at the mall, in the car, and on the bus. In the city, in the country, in the suburbs, in the Northeast, Southwest, West Coast, Alaska, Hawaii, and everywhere in between. Listening to Led Zep, Rush, Yes, Cream, Floyd, Skynyrd, Aerosmith, Genesis, Dead, Doobies, Doors, Who, Stones, Pistols, Sonny and Cher, Cheech and Chong, even Donny and Marie and Debby Boone—it all depended on musical taste, tang, flavor, choice, likes, and dislikes.

I'm simply here to inform, apprise, familiarize, report, and notify, not to judge, critique, surmise, assess, appraise, consider, or conclude.

Some will reminisce, remember, muse, ponder, reflect, recall, and recollect. Others may curse, gasp, ignore, frazzle, fume, avoid, or repress.

I'll just close my thesaurus and plead the fifth.

Dallas cow girls

88. Dallas Cowboy Cheerleaders

The Dallas Cowboy cheerleaders gave hormonally charged men and boys two more good reasons to forego lawn work on a Sunday afternoon. If the thrill of watching gridiron warriors hurt each other was not enough excitement for the average healthy American male, the scantily-clad cheerleaders shaking pom-poms and body parts made the NFL's allure an inescapable fact of life.

In Europe fans went to the stadium to cheer and brawl, in the U.S., to leer and drool.

89. Cheap Poster Thrills

Glance and twinge, then sigh and flip
Another card from the pile.
Sitting on Danny's carpet,
But staring at Farrah's smile.

Shuffle the deck and strain your neck
Dreaming about a date.
Posters around the bedroom
Make it hard to concentrate.

Still, just as planned you play your hand,
Trying to do your best.
But what's more important: a game of cards
Or a glance at Cheryl's chest?

The Seventies teenage bedroom
Caused many a boy to stare
At Farrah Fawcett's sexy pose,
With message in her hair.

We caught a glimpse of cleavage
Through the suit of Cheryl Ladd.
And Cheryl Tiegs' bikini
Was a sight that drove us mad.
The Dallas Cowboys' ladies,
In their outfits with the frills,
Gave way to dreams of passion
And hungry teenage thrills.
Charlie's gorgeous Angels—
Kate and Jaclyn Smith,
For active young libidos,
"Hey man, we plead the fifth."

Glance and twinge, then sigh and flip
Another poster rack.
The Nineties Spencer gift shop
Can give a heart attack.
Cindy Crawford shirtless.
Women drenched in sweat.
Men in string bikinis,
And you ain't seen nothing yet.
Clumps of naked bodies
Makes our generation chime:
"For sexual thrills in posters
We were born before our time . . ."

90. True Teen Confessions #2: Barry Manilow

"As a young teenage girl I was infatuated with Barry. You know Barry Manilow—that handsome man from New York City who wrote all those wonderful songs about love and special things. My entire life revolved around my little Copacabana Cutie. He was my reason for living. Every breath I took, I took for Barry. Every dream I dreamt, I dreamt for Barry. Every morsel of food I ate, I ate for Barry. Yes, he was my nourishment."

"There was no man on Earth who could ever compare. He was God's gift to womankind—a miracle. Listening to one of his songs elicited emotions that a young teenage girl of my upbringing was supposed to suppress. He seduced me with his soothing harmonies—always knowing what keys to stroke. His stimulating rhythms kept me grooving all night long. Barry's voice caressed my entire

Oh, Barry!

body sending me into a dancing frenzy. As the songs reached their climax, I screamed, 'Barry, it is magic, it is magic!'" *Well Barry, looks like we made it . . .*

"I was so crazy over Barry that I wanted to be his dog, Bagel. As Bagel, I could spend every second of my life with him. I could nuzzle up with Barry, pant all over him all night long, and lick his breakfast bowl clean in the morning. Then I'd sit on his lap and have him scratch behind my ears as I howled with ecstasy. Yes, if I were Bagel, all of Barry's affections would belong to me and I would not share him with any of the other dogs.

"I can see us spending a weekend in New England, walking hand-in-paw down the beach, with the waves crashing in and the sun setting. It would be so romantic, him walking along and me gently nipping his . . ."

"Uh . . . Excuse me, Ms. Benfer. I'm sorry, but our time's up for today's session. I think we've made some real progress. If you see my receptionist, Mandy, she'll schedule your appointment for next week."

91. Chinese Jump Rope

In it, out it, side-by-side it, on it, in it, out it . . .
Anklesies, calvesies, kneesies, thighsies . . .

92. The Impact of Watergate

It is said that the Watergate scandal ripped the political fabric of the United States, forever changing the way we view our national leaders and instilling a sense of moral self-doubt that pervaded our nation for more than a decade. This may be true, but Watergate committed a more unforgivable crime for the average twelve-year-old in 1973: it interrupted countless hours of daytime television.

It was the summer between sixth and seventh grade, a time when watching "Sale of the Century" (with Joe Garagiola) was a cherished daily ritual. Daytime game shows were my link to the outside world. We learned as much as we needed to know about current affairs by watching what model car Bob Barker was giving away on "The Price Is Right." Not to mention the educational value of seeing washed-up actors like Fannie Flagg, Brett

How do we turn him off?

Somers and Richard Paul on "The Match Game," "$1.98 Beauty Pageant," and "Tattletales" making sexual innuendos that went way over our heads. And "Password" did wonders for our vocabulary and verbal skills.

But the Watergate hearings changed all that. It wasn't that we objected to their being televised—we knew that someone somewhere was interested in all that political stuff. But why did they have to broadcast on EVERY CHANNEL? That, to me, was pure Communism.

For months instead of "What do you bid on the new Amana Radarange?" we got "So, Mr. Magruder, your involvement was limited to indirect exposure to the planning and execution of what you considered to be an isolated group of incidents wholly within the authority of the presidential advisory staff?'' It was maddening.

We tried to get involved and watch what was going on. We really did. But our idea of entertainment was a good sitcom plot that resolved itself within a half-hour, or someone ascending to win the grand prize of the day so she could become tomorrow's returning champion. In the Watergate hearings, nothing got resolved. And there were no fabulous prizes. If someone was winning and someone was losing, we could never tell.

It was nice when Nixon finally resigned the following year. He deserved it—not necessarily because of misdeeds he committed during his presidency, but because he was personally responsible for violating our right to daytime television.

93. The Colors of Our World—Part I

The colors of our world shape who we are, define our very purpose and path in life. The changing tide of time flows rapidly, from decade to decade, and with it comes dramatic shifts in the very fabric of life . . . or not.

1970s Colors	1990s Colors
Brown	Earthtone
Brown	Elm
Brown	Chocolate
Brown	Desert Sand
Brown	Chestnut
Brown	Ginger
Brown	Burnt Umber
Brown	Mocha

Brown	Oak
Brown	Lumber
Brown	Wheat
Brown	Mahogany
Brown	Bronze
Brown	Soil
Brown	Teak
Brown	Espresso

94. The Colors of Our World—Part II

Sears Kenmore appliances did severe damage to the landscape of America in the Seventies. Brian D. Ash, an electric stove engineer from Peoria, Illinois, actually conceptualized and concocted the first shades of "olive drab green," "puke yellow," and "mutated baby blue." In a 1974 interview with *Appliance World* magazine, Brian confessed that the true purpose for his creations was to mock and confuse his color-blind wife. Much to his surprise, the colors caught on and dramatically changed the face of American homes, clothing, and automobiles. Brian was last seen in 1982 driving south on the New Jersey Turnpike in an orange, two-tone, Oldsmobile Cutlass. His wife had left him a year earlier for a highway sign painter from Des Moines.

95. Schoolhouse Rock

"We the People, in Order to form a more perfect Union, establish Justice, insure domestic Tranquility,

provide for the common defence . . ." This is not just
an excerpt from the preamble to the United State's Constitution; ask anyone who woke up, poured themselves a
bowl of Coco Puffs, and planted themselves firmly in
front of the television on Saturday mornings during the
Seventies. These words from our nation's past are actually lyrics from the highly entertaining and now permanently ingrained "Schoolhouse Rock." These snippets
that appeared during commercial breaks on ABC did
more to educate America's youth than all of our primary
school English and History classes combined.

What year did the Civil War begin? Damned if I know.
What happened at the Battle of Saratoga? The battle of
who? But ask me how a bill becomes a law and watch the
floodgates open! *"I'm only a Bill, yes, I'm only a Bill
and I'm sitting here on Capitol Hill . . ."* I get a thrill
just thinking about it, psyched enough to use an *"Interjec-
tion, for excitement, or emotion, hallelujah, hallelujah,
hallelujah . . ."* Wait, how about *"Lolly, Lolly, Lolly get
your adverbs here . . ."* It's remarkable, and *"Conjunc-
tion Junction, what's your function?"* Ooh baby, don't
stop. Here, try another: Who was the 14th President of
the United States? *Ummmmmm . . .* "Schoolhouse
Rock" didn't cover that one. Search me. (Actually, you
can ask my friend, Jed, who learned all of the Presidents'
names in elementary school by singing them to the tune
of "Oh Christmas Tree" Ahem: "George Washington,
John Adams, Thomas Jefferson, James Madison, etc."
Thank you, Jed.)

Ideas for the nineties? Well, I have seen the "Schoolhouse Rock" videos for sale in one of those upscale
"learning accouterments for young persons" boutiques
(a.k.a. really pricey toy store) and I've noticed them
cropping up occasionally on Saturday morning. (Bravo,
ABC!) But I'm not sure of the appeal to today's kids.

Maybe something a little more contemporary, like Gangsta Rapper's ABC's . . . "A, E, I, O, U, little brotha/ Better learn those vowels/Better listen to your motha!" Or how about "Mathematical Metal" . . . "Aooough, baby yaow! Four times four equals 16, sweet sixteen, baby, do me now!" Maybe the "Red Hot Chili Professors" . . . "Stay in school, stay in school, stay in school, now!" You get the point. Get cracking, ABC! Isn't it time we steal Saturday morning back from the Ninja Turtles, Transformers and Mighty Morphin Power Rangers?

96. The Village People

97. Professional Sports Classroom, Lesson #1: Money Can't Buy Fans

In 1975, the management of the New York Cosmos of the North American Soccer League (NASL) offered Pelé a three-year, seven million dollar contract. In so doing, the Cosmos proved that no matter how much money you throw at a player, fans won't pay to watch an obscure game with funny rules. Pelé was considered to be the greatest soccer player in the world, but to the fans from Brooklyn he was "Peel, the little guy who can't use his hands."

And after hosting the 1994 World Cup, made possible by millions in U.S. corporate support, Americans could still only muster a mild, "Hey, desperate little guys running around trying to score . . . I got my fill of that in '77 at Studio 54."

98. Professional Sports Classroom, Lesson #2: Money Can't Buy Wins

George Steinbrenner and the Yankees proved Lesson #2 when, after two back-to-back World Series appearances, they spent $23 million to get Dave Winfield into pinstripes. The team then spent the next decade in the basement.

Of course, money is no longer an issue for Major League Baseball since the strike of '94 and '95 resolved all financial tensions: owners are happy, players are rich

and fans pay just $8.50 for a 10 ounce beer at the park.
Thanks, George.

99. TV Shows for the Undeserving

Proof that our priorities were out of line in the Seventies lies in the fact that Tony Orlando & Dawn had their
own television show. Think about it. Every week, a full
hour of music and variety, if you can call it that. And they
weren't the only group to achieve this pinnacle. Witness:
"The Sonny & Cher Comedy Hour," "The Marilyn
McCoo & Billy Davis, Jr., Show," "The Glen Campbell
Goodtime Hour," "Donny & Marie," "Sha Na Na" and
even "The Bobbie Gentry Show"—all were beamed into
our living rooms for at least one season. Each week,
there they were: singing, dancing and . . . well, at least
trying to act their hearts out. They were awful, and we
loved them.

It's hard to forget the "Tony Orlando & Dawn" set,
which featured huge cartoons of yellow ribbons tied
around (ole) oak trees—a reminder of the hit that catapulted them to fame and their own series. They were
supported by a chorus of actors and singers who per-
formed comedy sketches and musical numbers with
them. And it was a necessity for the stars to develop
"personalities" by trading insults with each other the
way that Sonny and Cher had done—Dawn (Joyce Vincent and Telma Hopkins) poked fun at Tony Orlando's
mustache; Marie picked on Donny's winning smile. It
was so cute. Like brothers and sisters would do. Like
"The Brady Bunch" would have done, and in fact *did* do

in their own short-lived variety series that took place on a set featuring—get ready if you forgot about this one—a giant swimming pool. The "Brady Variety Hour" was, arguably, the worst of them all.

Looking back, it's hard enough to believe that these people, many of whom are unhindered by talent of any kind, should have become famous. More unbelievable, though, is that someone at the network thought that by virtue of a hit song, these individuals could carry off a full hour of entertainment: Hey, it worked for Carol Burnett, right? What has she got that Jon "Bowzer" Bauman from Sha Na Na hasn't?

100. Jaws

Quite simply, *Jaws* made ocean swimming something we all thought twice about.

With good reason: sharks are big animals with big mouths and big teeth. Fear of them is natural.

And this fear offered the average late-night, beach-party stud an easy sobriety/availability test for potential scam targets:

Q: Wanna go skinnydipping? (Translation: Are you drunk enough to voluntarily submerge yourself in a medium that further slows your movements and dulls your senses, knowing that at anytime a hungry beast twice your size might attack from the murky depths and tear you to shreds?)

If "Yes," the subject was ripe. Further questioning was appropriate:

Q: Aren't the stars beautiful? (Translation: Is it so dark that you can't see my face?)

If "Yes," the deal was closed:

Q: Hi, I'm Elvis, how 'bout a hottub? (Translation: I'm Jerome, I'm sweaty, pimply, and fat.)

101. Mad Libs

The already hopelessly confused brains of America's children were further scrambled by *Mad Libs*—a game designed to construct oxymoronic stories by inserting random words into page-long short stories. Although *Mad Libs* helped reinforce the difference between adverbs and adjectives, it's most damaging effect was the complete subversion of truth and the abandonment of anything grounded in reality.

A (SECRET) LETTER FROM AN ADMIRER

Dear Miss [/Mr.] _____ ,
name of [person] in room

You may not recall my _____ , but I met
noun

you at the _____ cocktail party given
adjective

by our _____ friend, _____ .
adjective   *name*

We had a/an _____ talk about
adjective

_____ _____ , and I was
adjective   *plural noun*

impressed by your _____ conversation
adjective

and your grasp of the _____ situation.
adjective

Also, I was very much attracted by your

_____ eyes, your _____ little
adjective   *adjective*

chin, and your _____ teeth. If you'll
adjective

pardon me for seeming _____ , I was
adjective

fascinated by your _____ walk and by
adjective

your _____ figure.
adjective

I hope I made a/an _____ impression,
adjective

and that we can get together for a nice

_____ next week.
noun

                         _____ yours,
                            adverb

                     _____
                     name of [person] in room

From *The Original Mad Libs®©* 1958, 1982 by Price/Stern/Sloan Publishers, Inc., Los Angeles, CA 90048

Dear Mr. _Konsynski,_

You may not recall my _Schnauzer,_ but I met you at the _pus-filled_ cocktail party given by our _rancid_ friend, _Bitsy._ We had a/an _prickly_ talk about _pregnant tractor pulls,_ and I was impressed by your _moist_ conversation and your grasp of the _dietetic_ situation. Also, I was very much attracted by your _smelly_ eyes, your _poisonous_ little chin, and your _oozing_ teeth. If you'll pardon me for seeming _bloated,_ I was fascinated by your _dung-caked_ walk and by your _wood-paneled_ figure.

I hope I made a/an _molten_ impression, and that we can get together for a nice _dandruff_ next week.

Metallically yours,
Jonathan

102. Sears Toughskins

It was brutal. Not Levis, not even Wranglers, but Sears Toughskins jeans—the horrifying "X" tattooed on each rear pocket, a statement of pure "dorkdom," signifying the ultimate in uncool. Yes, they were less expensive. Yes, there was no perceivable difference in quality or fit. _But, c'mon Mom! They were Toughskins!_ It was clear that she didn't understand. Everyone who was anyone wore Levis—it was the key to normal teenage existence. People who didn't wear Levis were destined to a lower status, a life of ridicule and despair. (The phrase "inferiority complex" was actually coined in a Kansas City boy's department fitting room during the September 1975 Sears "back to school" sale.)

Despite Mom's perception, there were no real advantages, no real cost savings; the extra five bucks she saved in the short term would be spent years later to pay for extensive psychotherapy. Overcoming the Toughskins stigma is truly a lifelong process; believe me, I know. Those of us branded as "Toughskins Teens" vowed to never suffer again, vowed to end our shame and humiliation, to finally silence the deafening "*vvvht . . . vvvht . . . vvvht . . .*" sound they made when the cheap denim rubbed against cheap denim as we walked. As soon as we gained our shopping independence, we flocked to the malls, ravenously stalking our sacred Levis, attempting to instantly cleanse ourselves and establish new places in society. Some went even further than Levis, staging stronger rebellions against their sordid pasts. Calvin Klein, Jordache, Sasson, Chic, Gloria Vanderbilt, and even Bugle Boy were direct outgrowths of this phenomenon, weapons of retaliation for the resentful youth of America.

By the early Nineties, I thought I had finally left my past behind, that I had healed my Toughskins wounds and landed on my feet. I had found stability, comfortably sporting my Levi's 501s and designer shirts, strolling through life as I had always dreamed, feeling proud, quoting Dana Carvey's "Saturday Night Live" impression of George Michael—"Look at my butt! Look at it!" I had that glorious Levi's heritage stitched into my back pockets for all the world to see; I was invincible! And then, without warning, it happened . . . I walked into the GAP and quickly discovered that they no longer carried Levis! The salesperson asked, "would you like to try on a pair of our own plain pocket jeans?" My response was immediate, fierce and aggressive, as if she was threatening my very existence, "No, and I never will!" I stormed out of the store, vowing never to return. I was frightened by my behavior, by my brutal attack of this salesperson. My carefully repressed Toughskins trauma had resurfaced. I'm okay now, but I live in fear. Perhaps someday we will understand the deep-rooted psychosis of the Seventies Toughskins teen, but until that time, we must be on our guard. Comrades: stay close to your 501s, and retail clerks: beware.

103. Mr. October and the "Reggie" Bar

On October 18, 1977, Reggie Jackson put three baseballs in three pitches over the fence during the sixth and last World Series game against the Dodgers. The implication: save your allowance, buy tickets to the game, go to the park, and meet Reggie.

On February 22, 1978, Reggie Jackson and Stanford Brands introduced *Reggie!*—the 25¢ two-ounce "chocolaty covered caramel and peanuts" bar. The implication: it's easier to watch the game on the couch, suck down a couple of cans of soda, and eat Reggie.

104. R.I.F. Reading Is Funky

For those of you who only read *Tiger Beat, Teen Beat, 'Teen, Seventeen, MAD, Cracked, National Lampoon, Rock, Ri¢hie Ri¢h, The Hair Bear Bunch,*

The Funky Phantom, Sad Sack, Beetle Bailey, G.I. Combat, Kamandi: The Last Boy on Earth, The Archies, O'Malley and the Alley Cats, Chip 'n' Dale, and on and on . . . see what classics you missed.

A Book Report: Seventies Bestsellers

1. The Female Orgasm: Psychology, Physiology, Fantasy by Dr. Seymour Fisher. (Basic Books, Inc.) *Found in Mom's bureau drawer under the girdles and junk. What's up doc? How come you know so much about female orgasms? Either you've got a very liberal research grant or you're a pretty funky guy or your operation in Sweden was a total success.*

2. The Joy of Sex by Dr. Alex Comfort. (Crown Books) *Found in Dad's drawer under the Fruit of the Looms and Playboys. The drawings helped to explain a lot. But, two questions still linger. What's with the armpit hair and where does this Comfort guy hang out? Certainly not at the local Dairy Queen. And what joy? Seventies teenage males remember sex—or the pursuit of sex—to be painful, full of humiliation and rejection, lying and trying, conjecture and torture, nocturnal emissions and plea conditions. "Keep hope alive."*

3. Our Bodies, Ourselves by The Boston Women's Health Book Collective. (Simon & Schuster) *Because stupid brothers were too busy looking through their parent's drawers trying to unravel the mysteries of the opposite sex, they left their sister's drawers alone. If they had ventured through them, they would have seen this book, handed from mother to daughter, and learned the truth about the female body. But then again, maybe they found it and flipped through it, but* put it back because there were only a few explicit drawings. *(Brothers, I swear. What a bunch of dorks!)*

4. Our Wonderful World: An Encyclopedic Anthology for the Entire Family. (Grolier) *Mom bought it in the supermarket, one volume per week. Plagiarize. Plagiarize. Plagiarize. Face it—there was no way to get caught. You never saw this book in the school library (and the teachers had no idea it existed). But, there it was on your shelf, thanks to Mom and FoodTown. If you ever wanted a prefabricated essay on Hernando Cortez, planets, Beowulf, or hundreds of other topics, simply open up to the page and start copying. No problem. Tons better than Cliff Notes.*

5. Alive: The Story of the Andes Survivors by Piers Paul Read. (Lippincott) *Excellent high school book report action. The gripping and wicked awesome story of plane crash survivors who resort to cannibalism to stay alive. Imagine splitting open skulls with axes and carving out the brains, and cooking a stew by mixing the brains with various vital organs. Good food for thought.*

6. Where Do Babies Come From? by Margaret Sheffield and Sheila Bewley. (Alfred A. Knopf, Inc.) *Myth shattering book complete with colorful artist's renderings showing exactly where babies come from. No longer can we trust the schoolyard origination versions of the vegetable stand at the local Stop & Shop, the stork, the milkman, and the belly button on Mommy's tummy (and the subject was dropped at that point because the thought was too gross).*

7. Jonathan Livingston Seagull by Richard Bach. (Macmillan) *When we first read about Jonathan the*

*Seagull, we marvelled at the profound, almost mysti-
cal, undercurrents of his simple dialogue as he spoke
with the other seagulls. His messages were clear:
individuality was to be maintained by listening and
following your voice, making your own rules, and
staying true to your vision despite the peer pressure.
This was pretty heavy, especially at a time when we all
strived to wear the same elephant bellbottoms. However, after the second reading of the ninety-three page
book, we immediately thought: A talking seagull . . .
Give us a break!*

**8. Helter Skelter: The True Story of the Manson
Murders** by Vincent Bugliosi with Curt Gentry. (W.W.
Norton & Company) *We don't want to write anything
about this book. Charles Manson may get paroled.*

9. Fear of Flying by Erica Jong. (Holt, Rinehart and
Winston) *No wonder Isadora Wing had a fear of flying.
Who wouldn't after the movies* Airport, Airport 1975,
Airport '77, *and* Airport '79: The Concorde? *With
crazed bombers, private planes crashing into cockpits,
hijackers who force the plane to crash in the Bermuda
Triangle, cruise missiles . . . I'd have a fear of flying
too!*

10. The Complete Book of Running, by Jim Fixx.
(Random House) *Avoid this book and let this fad pass.
You already know how to run, if you have to. The
Adidas sneakers and designer polyester running outfits will only end up in the closet, unused, after a week.
Why? Television and Screaming Yellow Zonkers!
prove too tempting. So spare your muscles the excru-
ciating pain, keep your body flabby, and save yourself
the price of the book. With the savings, buy a case of*

Schlitz beer, sit back in your worn lounge chair, and exercise your drinking arm.

105. "Don't put that in your mouth!" Three Rumors That Changed the Meaning of Ingestion Forever.

"Mikey" and the Pop Rock Mishap

When the rumors of Mikey's death hit the junior high lunchroom, there was little concern or bereavement—just a healthy rekindling of interest in the scientific method:

"Petey just heard it from Daniel who said that Zachrey's mom heard that Mikey—you know, Mikey from "Hey Mikey, he liked it"—ate too many Pop Rocks on a dare, then drank a soda and . . . *wham!* Exploded!"

"Man, that must have been messy with all those Pop Rocks fizzing in his stomach juice. Grody."

"I bet Walter the Black Hole hasn't heard yet. You get all the Pop Rocks you can find, and I'll get the soda."

"What are we going to do, man?"

"Watch the black hole super nova."

"Awwright!"

The Alice Cooper Guaranteed-to-Gross-You-Out Spittoon Story

In an effort to whip his adolescent crowd into a primeval fervor, Alice Cooper was rumored to have passed a jug through the audience challenging them to create a "Cooper Cocktail."

"I heard French kissing means passing spit."

"That's nothing, man, didya hear about Alice Cooper. He passed a bucket around at a concert and had everybody hawk big old loogies and clams in there. Then they brought it back up on stage and he drank like two gallons of it before he barfed."

"That's *way worse* than french kissing, man."

"You said it."

The Legend of A Rock Star—Who Shall Remain Nameless for Legal Reasons (but we all know who he is . . .)

Only a certain sexy male rock star's gastroenterologist really knows the truth, but the alleged story of this star's pre-performance perquisites have been told and retold so many times that the tale is getting hard to swallow. In its definitive and final form, the legend substantiates the discovery of three gallons of semen, an undisclosed number of assorted color condoms, and a man who calls himself "Jonah" hidden in the recesses of the star's innards. Although this whale was not called "Moby," it seems "Dick" played a role somewhere in this story.

106. John Travolta

It wasn't a note from Juan Epstein's mother. It wasn't Arnold Horshack's "Ooo, Ooo" or Freddie "Boom Boom" Washington's "Mr. Kot-Tair" that caught our attention. It was Vinnie Barbarino . . .

"Whut?"

That's right. Vinnie Barbarino. The sexiest Sweathog of them all. Even the almighty Fonz couldn't touch him.

"Welcome Back, Kotter" hit the airwaves, and John Travolta emerged as king.

And what do Brooklyn royalty wear on Saturday night? Why a princely white leisure suit, of course. It made

Travolta in the pose that shaped a decade

perfect sense—dress Vinnie up in his weekend best, plop him on a flashing dance floor, shine lights on a mirror ball and pump in Bee Gees disco music. Why not make a movie? What could go wrong?

Well, frankly, everything. Chaos. Utter, uncontrollable lunacy. John Travolta's break from television onto the big screen opened the floodgates of Seventies hell. The nation worshipped the disco frenzy of *Saturday Night Fever*, sucking the last remnants of rationality and good taste from American culture.

Was it Travolta's fault? Not really. He didn't ask for super-stardom. He didn't force us to gyrate our hips and wear platform shoes. He didn't see how Vinnie Barbarino's dim-witted mind reflected the general blunted aptitude of American society. Travolta simply stumbled forward, blinded by success.

Sweathog. Tony Manero, disco deity. *The Boy in the Plastic Bubble*. Danny Zuko in *Grease*. What more can be said? It's almost pointless to explore the damage caused by John Travolta. His finger-pointing pose is the absolute icon of Seventies culture, the most poignant image and most potent reminder of our generation's curse. Still, one has to respect Travolta's judgment. He restrained his astonishing power, saving society from perils unknown. Just imagine how much worse it could have been if John had let his ego run amok; be thankful about what *didn't* happen in the Seventies:

"Saturday Night Fever," the prime time television series.

"Saturday Morning Fever," the animated cartoon series.

Saturday Night Fever II, the movie sequel (although John did try again in 1983 with *Stayin' Alive*, but by then it was too late).

"Saturday Night Fever," the board game with lighted dance floor.

"Saturday Night Fashion," the Macy's leisure suit collection.

"Travolta," fragrance for men.

"More Than A Woman," fragrance for women.

"Jivin' John" disco dance schools.

"Tony Manero" the 12-inch doll with blow-dried hair.

"Fever Crunch" breakfast cereal.

---

13 Uncool Things

13. Toughskins jeans.
12. Bringing a bag lunch to school, and even uncooler, bringing lunch to school in a "Brady Bunch" lunch box, complete with a thermos.
11. Two-tone carpeting that covers the entire ground floor of the house, regardless of the room, and has several animal urine stains here and there.
10. Neil Diamond.
9. McDonald's Fish Sandwiches.
8. Birthday parties with your teenage friends thrown by Mom.
7. Having your parents pick you up after school in the family wood-paneled station wagon.
6. Anything religious.
5. The Osmonds.
4. Big, oozing, corpulent zits.
3. Violin lessons.
2. Younger brothers.
1. Horse meat.

Let your imagination run wild and then shudder. We would still be wearing floral polyester today if not for an element of restraint in our national hero of the Seventies. John Travolta: we curse you and thank you in the same breath. *Pulp Fiction* was cool—It was strange, yet somehow comforting, to see you up there on the big screen in such a big way. Welcome back. Sorry about the Oscar. Better luck next year.

107. The Silly Straw

To a child intrigued by the laws of nature, the Silly Straw was an experiment.

To a parent trying to teach a child good table manners, the Silly Straw was Satan.

108. Seventies Slang

We apologize for the constantly overused words "wicked" and "cool." We tried to add variety to our adjectives, we really did. But we failed. However, we hope you understand it's not our fault. We grew up during a bland and unimaginative decade. We clung to TV shows to develop our vocabulary with Richie Cunningham's "Sit on it" or Fonzie's "hhhaaayyy" or Arnold Horshack's "Ooo . . . Ooo . . ." or Vinnie Barbarino's "Whut?" or J.J. Walker's "Dy-no-mite!" or even Kojak's "Who loves ya, baby?" We relied on the "Blaxploitation" movies to deliver such gems as "dig it," "right on," and "hang loose sugar." And we relied on our older siblings to pass on "Dahhh?" "neat," "hey, man," "no shit, Sherlock," and "dreamy." Luckily the West Coast added "totally psyched." But even these words weren't enough to deliver us from "wicked cool" or "wicked awesome!"

How do the kids of today do it? How do they create all of these words? And what do they mean? *Homeboy* . . . Is their "homeboy" our John Boy? The word *kickin* on the playground back in the Seventies meant kicking the red rubber ball. *Bitchin* means people complaining, right? *Def* . . . Eh? What did you say? *Chillin* means you're cold and it's time to put on the corn cob jacket. *Fly* . . . Like maybe you're flying low around the equator? *Righteous* . . . Well, there were no righteous people from the Seventies. *Barney and Betty* . . . They were Fred and Wilma's friends, right? A *tubular* was used to float in the granite quarry. *Word* . . . Like "word to your mother." Poor Mom. She deserves more than one word. *Bodacious* . . . What the hell is a bodacious? When did *man* become *dude?* *Totally rad* . . . Don't they mean *bad?* And then all of a sudden *bad* became good, or is bad still bad . . .

We of the Seventies generation appear before you utterly confused, and . . . *wicked* depressed.

109. Mind Purge

A young man steps into a Winnebego as a mere mortal and then emerges as the all powerful Shazam. A young woman utters the words "Oh mighty Isis" and gains untold superhero powers. The fact that our generation remembers these things frightens us. There are many more important subjects to take up valuable brain space. Isn't it time to clear the "Shazam-Isis Hour" out of our memory banks? No wonder we can't concentrate. How can we focus on solving our nation's problems when the lyrics to "Bohemian Rhapsody" are clogging up our heads? How can we achieve world peace with the titles of Wacky Pack stickers taking up valuable cranium space. C'mon folks! Let's let some of these useless memories go! Here's a list to start with:

- Positions of all the Bradys in the grid
- Names of the Jackson 5
- Names of the Osmond brothers
- Anything having to do with the TV series "Phyllis"
- Rules to the board game Which Witch
- "Shazbat" and any other "Morkisms"
- Zoom "ubby-dubby" talk
- Theme song to "Alice"
- Gerald Ford's presidency

- How to blow-dry and feather your hair
- How to fold those stupid paper finger devices that flipped back and forth and held messages inside
- The entire bicentennial celebration
- Host Gene Rayburn on "The Match Game"
- Luke and Laura
- Plots of all "Scooby Doo" episodes
- Ability to "walk the dog" with Duncan butterfly yo-yo
- *Sergeant Pepper's Lonely Hearts Band* starring Peter Frampton and the Bee Gees
- Doing arithmetic without a calculator
- Raj, Rerun and Dwayne on "What's Happening!!"
- Drinking legally at age 18
- Sylvester Stallone drinking raw eggs in *Rocky*
- Juan Luis Pedro Phillipo de Huevos Epstein
- All the response lines, plus throwing rice and toilet paper at *Rocky Horror*
- Grammar
- "Hee-Haw"
- Lawrence Welk
- Rotary dial telephones
- The Friday-night lineup: (8:00 "Brady Bunch," 8:30 "The Partridge Family," 9:00 "Room 222," 9:30 "The Odd Couple," 10:00 "Love, American Style")
- Wacky Racers
- Typewriters
- Where to buy blacklight bulbs
- Dance steps to the Latin Hustle
- Using a protractor
- How to properly clean the dust off records
- All CB radio lingo
- *Two all-beef patties . . .*

110. It Never Ends

It is impossible to end this book at one hundred and thirteen, but we are physically unable to continue much longer. The memories are too overwhelming. The physical signs of our combat stress are all here. Jay K., whose voice is beginning to crack, plays the B-sides of his 45s over and over and over. Scott, in between his migraines and occasional bouts of nausea, incessantly and involuntarily repeats Marcia's lines from old "Brady" episodes. Tamara is playing with her dolls again, still trying to make Skipper's breasts grow even larger. Jay S. is still at the mall shopping for the perfect candle. And Greg. Well Greg has dusted off the old Huffy and is going for the nine barrel record, but this time he'll wear a cup!

Hopefully these signs of stress aren't showing up in you as well. However, as you read through this book you probably remembered hundreds of additional trivial bits of memories, facts and fictions. That is why we created this crossword puzzle to test your Seventies trivial knowledge and to suggest more nouns (people, places, or things) that screwed up our generation.

Have fun, good luck, and may you take this book to your shrink (or better yet, buy another copy as a gift) so he or she can better understand you.

The answers are on page 215.

Down

1. The Blues Brothers: Jake and ___
2. Baxter and Knight
4. Uganda's President-for-Life Idi ___
5. "The Night Chicago ___"
7. Henry Winkler's Ivy League alma mater
8. Patty Hearst's SLA name
9. Erica Jong's *Fear of* ___
10. ___Fischer defeated Russian Boris Spassky in chess
11. Nixon's tape-erasing secretary ___ Woods
15. A James Taylor album
16. Suzanne *Zuma Beach* ___
17. Toxic pollutant sprayed on Mexican cannabis
19. Ali MacGraw's real first name
20. Evelyn "___" King
23. *Moment by Moment* star, not John Travolta
26. Jim Fixx's fixation
29. Jimmy Smiley's mother, Miss ___
30. Cosby's Fat ___
33. Burt, prison, football, ball in crotch, and *The Longest* ___
36. Al ___'s #1 song, "Let's Stay Together"
37. Csonka, Kiick, and Warfield left this NFL town to join the WFL
40. The Jackson who was born right before Michael
41. The plumpest Jackson
42. The oldest Jackson-Five member
43. The most talented Jackson with a pet rat
44. National Organization of Women
46. Tonka ___
47. The Onassis island

49. All this Ali-beating boxer wants for Christmas is his two front teeth
51. Joey Travolta's movie debut
52. Mary Richard's TV station's initials
54. LeVar Burton played __ __ in *Roots*
56. The Partridge Family agent, Reuben __
59. David "the dog told me to do it" Berkowitz, a.k.a. __ __ __
61. Norman "Stanley Roper" __
63. Wilt "the Stilt" __
64. Alice's *special friend*, __, the butcher
66. Top Cat
67. Ohio Congressperson Wayne Hays and his secretary Elizabeth
69. *SNL's* producer __ Michaels
70. Meredith Baxter loves David __
71. John Lennon's *Plastic* wife
73. "Set a course for adventure . . ." on the __ __
74. Barbie's neutered boyfriend
76. Broadway Joe Namath's last NFL team before retiring
77. "One Way Or Another" she will get you . . . you wished
78. Vanilla Ice is to M.C. Hammer as the __ were to the J-5
81. Stallone's dud following *Rocky*
82. __*the Cat*, XXX
85. Rose "__ Wash" Royce
87. Intrauterine device
89. "Ten-four good buddy"

Across

3. Teenage Triple Crown jockey Steve __
6. The Manson follower, __"Squeaky" Fromme, who shot Ford
9. Dean Wormer's college, where "Knowledge is good"
12. Brooke Shields as __ Nevada
13. __ "You Make Me Feel Like Dancing" Sayer
14. The firefighting Buffalo Bill
18. Pamela Sue Martin as __ Drew
21. "__" by Boston
22. __ Ziffel, Schwarzenegger, Horshack
24. The one Gibb who was *not* a Bee Gee
25. __-DeeToo
27. The __ Spitfire

28. The Goodbye Girl little kid, __ Cummings
31. Philippe __, the French playboy who married Princess Caroline
32. Jimmy's beer brewing brother
34. __ *Fools Die* Puzo
35. Tall blond + Stallone + Dudley Moore + mattress = Susan __
38. Nipsey Russell played the __ in *The Wiz*
39. Equal Rights Amendment
42. The one Jackson who stayed with Motown
45. Amy Carter's dog
48. Adam "Goody Two Shoes" __
50. The Orkan
53. Smokey's hit, "Tears of a __"
55. Rerun time: Batperson and Robin, the Dynamic __
56. Bald headed, Tootsie sucking cop
57. " __, ho, ho, it's magic!"
58. Manfred __
59. Jon Bauman of __
60. Mork saying, "goodbye"
62. Scotland's shy __ __ Monster
65. Black private dick + sex machine =
68. Official soft drink of the Moscow Olympics
70. Native American + karate fighter = __ Jack
72. __ Conn sang the movie soundtrack, "You Light Up My Life"
75. Morris *"Feeeeeelings"* __
79. The Godfather, Don Vito __
80. Scott Baio's memorable gangster flick, *Bugsy* __
82. Oscar Madison's odd roommate
83. Partridge and Bonaduce
84. __ __. Agnew
86. Marcus Welby, __
88. Steve "King __" Martin
89. Sissy Spacek + John Travolta + Stephen King + bucket of pig's blood = __
90. " __ and the Sea Monsters"
91. Travolta's *Grease* hood, Danny __
92. World's first test-tube baby Louise, or the official Seventies color
93. The Saturday morning test from high school hell

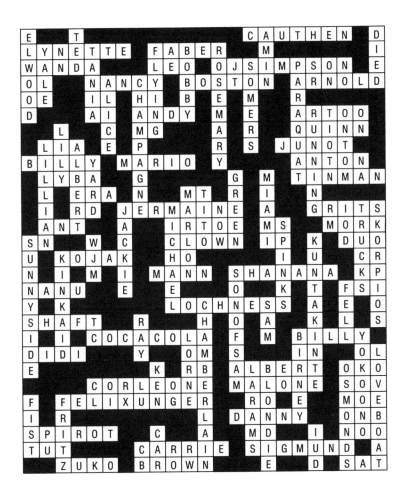

111. A Very Brady Conclusion

American youth fought desperately for liberty during
the late-Sixties. They turned on, dropped out, cranked
Hendrix and finally broke free from the suburban estab-
lishment that was called the United States. A mighty

victory had been won. The God-given right to acid rock and free expression had finally been recognized.

Then, the tie-died youth of the Sixties passed on this blessing of liberty to us, the children of the Seventies. We warmly accepted their offering and praised its worth, rejoicing in the fact that we were now free to do whatever we wanted. But like the aqua-blue ceramic bowls people receive for wedding presents, we weren't quite sure what to do with our new gift. Unlike our Sixties counterparts, we had very little to worry about in the Seventies. The Vietnam war was ending, the Civil Rights movement had moved on, there were no new drugs. All the great battles had already been fought; we were left only to languish in the boring aftermath, uttering "Okay, now what?" Our generation began to flounder, trying to find some legitimate use for this boundless freedom we had been granted.

We tried to care about Watergate, but couldn't. The scandal was way above our heads and certainly out of our control; we let our parents read the newspapers and watch the evening news while we retreated to our rooms, trying to find something better to be concerned about. There we sat, each of us, alone, staring at our blacklight-postered walls, trying to find something, anything, to bind us together as a generation. Then it came to us, one by one, over the syndicated airwaves—a presence that was unique, a force that we could truly call our own. We clung to it, worshipped it, revered its name and chanted its anthem . . .

"The Brady Bunch."

It rose high above the sea of fads and fashions that confused our decade. Mike, Carol, Marcia, Greg, Jan,

Peter, Cindy, Bobby, and Alice. They called out to us, uniting the desperate youth of the Seventies. It wasn't much, but hey, it was ours, all ours.

We craved for problems, and the Bradys had them. Marcia's braces, Jan's imaginary phone boyfriend, Peter's changing vocal chords, Bobby's height—granted the dilemmas were not earthshattering and were always solvable in less than thirty minutes, but still, we took what we could get. Then a fascinating interplay of forces began; we eagerly watched and thirsted for more problems, yet at the same time, our patience dwindled; any issue that couldn't be addressed quickly and painlessly became intolerable. The effect of "The Brady Bunch" was truly dramatic, as our generation settled into a schedule of Friday night insta-solve predicaments. The aftershock of this transformation can be felt even today, as our societal addiction to instant food and instant communication grows out of control. We are an impatient, quick and dirty generation.

But "The Brady Bunch" represented much more than a new problem solving mindset for misguided youth. Unfortunately for the editors of *Vogue* and *GQ,* many elements of Seventies fashion came directly out of Brady closets and dresser drawers. Specifics are too painful to discuss, but much of the blame for plaid bellbottoms and floral polyester can be placed upon Sherwood Schwartz (the "Brady" creator) and his team of sadistic costume designers. And the damage doesn't end there . . .

"The Brady Bunch" symbolized the unspoken, disturbed sexual fantasies of our generation. The swinging singles scene and free love society that surrounded us was off limits, so we let our imaginations run wild through the innocent setting of the Brady household. No one spoke about it, but everybody knew . . . Greg and Marcia sharing the same bathroom through five years of puberty; it was every teenager's dream, living in such close quarters with a sexy, non-blood relative . . . You could even see the twinkle in their eyes if you looked closely enough.

The Bradys also elicited a more innocent and sincere level of envy. In real life, older brothers and sisters could only dream of receiving the amount of respect and adoration that Greg and Marcia got from their younger siblings. Likewise, younger siblings could never get the kind of attention and nonviolent behavior from their older counterparts. We all secretly wished that our own self-centered, blow-drier crazy, Camaro-worshiping siblings could show the same level of love, support, and respect as the Brady kids.

In short, "The Brady Bunch" fulfilled our needs, feeding us when we were hungry for purpose in life. They provided the problems, the solutions, the dreams, and the fantasies for an entire generation. The awkward adolescence of the show was a metaphor for our generation, sandwiched between the "childhood" rebellion of the Sixties and the "young adult—yuppie" materialism of the Eighties. The Seventies can be personified by a zit-faced, lanky, fourteen-year-old, trying desperately to fit into his/her confusing and changing world.

Despite the serious undertones of our Brady obsession, we of the twentysomething generation developed an uncanny ability to laugh at ourselves. We truly knew that we were a pathetic lot, never taking anything, especially "The Brady Bunch," too seriously. It is this quality that has paved the way for *Stuck in the Seventies,* allowing us to relish in the glorious yet painful absurdity of our younger years. We share both fondness and nausea as we explore the decade that has shaped us, and share a sense of both pride and doom as we watch today's youth make the same mistakes we did. To our

Eighties and Nineties counterparts, we pass on the gift of freedom we received from our Sixties predecessors, as well as our knowledge and insight about the Seventies. We offer simple words of advice: Please think very seriously before trying on a leisure suit or platform shoes. Please listen cautiously to any new music with a bumping, disco beat. And finally, remember—*The Brady Bunch Movie* might *seem* real, but it's not. We know. We were there . . .

. . . and it wasn't *that* bad.

112.

"G'Night, John Boy . . ."

113.

The '70s Little Instruction Book
113 groovy instructions to make you smile

Follow these 113 groovy cool little instructions and live the life of a Brady.

1. Do it.
2. Do the Hustle.
3. Don't swim in the ocean off Amity Island, especially if you hear a cello's "dah-dah, dah-dah."
4. Never mix Pop Rocks and Coca Cola. Remember Mikey from Life Cereal?
5. The next time a car cuts you off, yell "Kiss my grits!"
6. Sit in the middle of the theater for Sensurround movies.
7. Rock the Boat.
8. Turn on with TM.
9. Keep the tips of your wide ties three inches above your navel.
10. Keep the tips of your Elvis lamb chop sideburns three inches below your ear lobe.
11. Ho, ho, ho, it's magic, *never* believe *it's* not *so.*
12. Lay down, Sally.
13. In life's little battles, go 15 rounds like Rocky Balboa.
14. Don't be a hero, especially if your name is Billy.
15. Rescue a rock from the ground that is deserving of a good home, instead of bringing home a boxed pet.

16. Don't call chicks, babes.
17. Never admit to being a Riggs pig.
18. Lay down and boogie and play that funky music till you die.
19. Be careful around school buses painted in groovy-cool psychedelic squares because nervous mothers are driving.
20. Fly like an eagle.
21. Just remember that, it's a grand illusion, deep inside we're all the same.
22. The next time your boss pisses you off, tell him to "Sit on it."
23. Don't fly in an airplane piloted by George Kennedy.
24. Keep on truckin'.
25. Stay away from guys nicknamed Bad, Bad, Leroy Brown.
26. Beep, beep, yer ass.
27. May the Force be with you.
28. Remember the night Chicago died.
29. Be a Macho, Macho-Man.
30. Take the money and run.
31. Use Nair for short-shorts.
32. Elephant bell-bottoms must have a diameter of at least eight inches.
33. True platform shoes have at least five inch heels.
34. Don't tell your friends that Davey Jones will be your junior high school prom date until he actually says "Yes."
35. You are strong. You are invincible. You are woman. Roar.

36. Macrame away the tension.
37. Boogie oogie oogie.
38. Tell Brandy she's a fine girl.
39. Tell the person you love, "Let's get it on," in a voice deeper than Barry White's.
40. Do yourself a favor and don't tell your wife to "stifle yourself."
41. Fly, Robin, fly.
42. Do the Timewarp.
43. Don't go breakin' my heart.
44. Avoid people named Damian with 666 etched in their skull.
45. Don't throw lawn darts at loved ones.
46. When your mood ring is black, it's broken—return it.
47. Let it be.
48. Don't even try to learn the metric system.
49. Zoom a zoom a zoom a zoom . . .
50. Take it to the limit.
51. Learn the truth at 17.
52. Befriend people named Carrie.
53. Grab a little afternoon delight.
54. Toga! Toga! Toga!
55. Fully extend your arms when playing with clackers to avoid eye loss.
56. Play Marquis de Sade and zap a bug electronically.
57. Stay inside the next time the lights go out in Georgia.
58. Avoid bridges names Tallahatchi or Verrazano.

59. Baby, baby, don't get hooked on him.
60. Knock three times on the ceiling if you love someone or if they're playing Led Zeppelin too loudly.
61. Have some joy, have some fun, have some seasons in the sun.
62. Get down, tonight.
63. Blondes have more fun.
64. Two out of three ain't bad.
65. Grease is the word.
66. Find another couple and swing.
67. Watch out for falling Skylab debris.
68. Don't drink Kool-Aid served by a reverend in Guyana.
69. Avoid super freaks.
70. Practice the phrase, "Voulez-vous couchez avec moi ce soir?"—you never know when it might come in handy.
71. Be a dancing, dancing, dancing machine.
72. Love is thicker than water.
73. Knock on wood.
74. Go AWOL and desert the KISS Army.
75. Make sure you have expert timing when you're Kung-fu fighting.
76. Avoid killer bees.
77. Shed your clothes and streak.
78. Stop wishing for bionic implants.
79. Come on, ease on down, ease on down the road.
80. Use brown shag carpeting to complement virtually any decor.

81. Avoid all natural fabrics and fibers.
82. Guys: you can't go wrong with a powder blue tux at the prom.
83. If you find a great shampoo, be sure to tell two friends—who can each tell two friends, and so on, and so on . . .
84. You don't have to need something in order to go to a mall.
85. If you experience "Night Fever," take two aspirin and call the Boogie Doctor in the morning.
86. If you haven't found love, don't worry—cruise director Julie McCoy will fix you up.
87. Don't try jogging without a good $50 pair of Puma jogging shoes, preferably blue suede with orange stripes.
88. Never reveal what comes between you and your Calvins.
89. Be proud to be a Sweathog.
90. Always remember who loves ya, baby.
91. Watch out—it might not be a quarter, it might be one of those new Susan B. Anthony dollars.
92. A puka shell necklace goes with almost any outfit.
93. We must, we must, we must improve the bust.
94. Give a hoot—don't pollute.
95. Remember to unplug your lava lamp before you go to bed.
96. If you can't be with the one you love, honey, love the one you're with.

97. Don't give up on us, baby.
98. Book 'em, Danno.
99. Find paradise by the dashboard light.
100. Wish upon a star.
101. There's got to be a morning after.
102. If someone makes you an offer you can't refuse, take it.
103. No Coke, Pepsi.
104. Don't open the door when someone answers "Land Shark."
105. There are 50 ways to leave your lover.
106. You can check out any time you want, but you can never leave.
107. Whip Inflation Now with a button.
108. Love hurts.
109. Get the Knack.
110. Dim all the lights, sweet, darlin'.
111. Please don't go.
112. There are two paths you can go by, but in the long run, there's still time to change the road you're on.
113. Smile.

About the Authors

The authors have the distinction of being irreversibly damaged by childhoods that occurred in the 1970s.

Jay Kerness, a Chicago advertising executive, is dreaming up slogans to burn up O.P.E.C. oil and make land barges hot again. He is also testing the waters of musical lunacy by writing, composing and producing off-Broadway late night theater in New York City.

Tamara Nikuradse, a marketing director for a New York City cosmetics firm, is pushing the R&D department to develop a *wicked cool* robin's egg blue line of cosmetics and a mood lipstick that changes colors with emotions (only one problem though, the color keeps coming up black).

Scott Matthews, a vice president at a New York City book publisher, is hanging out at landfills searching for the next Jonathan Livingston Seagull (although this time there will be a book, a Saturday morning cartoon and an interactive Seagull CD). Scott and Tamara, a swinging married couple, co-authored 12 books, including the ultimate atonements for all our '70s sins, *Dear Mom: Thank You For Being Mine* and *Dear Dad: Thank You For Being Mine.*

Jay Steele, a procurement executive with a Silicon Valley high-tech firm, is working to bring *Son of Pong* to TV sets everywhere. He has recently drawn upon his fine '70s education (largely from ABC's "Grammar Rock") to co-write another humor book, *Practical Prayers for the Modern World,* which will be in bookstores the spring of 1996.

And **Greg White** is hoping to bring back those tight 100% polyester shirts that cling to your back, glue to the sweat under your arms and cause minor skin irritation. Just by chance, he's the guy in charge of sales and marketing for a fan and air conditioner company outside Boston.